STONE AGE SOUNDTRACKS

THE ACOUSTIC ARCHAEOLOGY OF ANCIENT SITES

Paul Devereux

vega

A catalogue record for this book is available
from the British Library.

ISBN 1-84333-019-9

Printed in Great Britain
by CPD, Wales

© Vega 2001

A member of the Chrysalis Group plc

First published in 2001 by
Vega
64 Brewery Road
London, N7 9NY

Visit our website at www.chrysalisbooks.co.uk

Project manager: *Stuart Booth*
Copy editor: *Christopher Westhorp*
Design: *Blacks Design*

Contents

Acknowledgements

First and foremost, I wish to thank the following for their exceptional kindness in supplying me with pictures, permissions or information – and sometimes all three – at very short notice: Lya Dams, Marlene Dobkin di Rios, Rauno Lauhakengas, Arnold Lettieri Jr, Tahir Shah and Aaron Watson.

I am grateful for the support offered by my colleagues in the International Consciousness Research Laboratories (ICRL) group, especially Robert Jahn and Brenda Dunne. (Special note is also made of ICRL Research Fellow Ian Cook's work on mind-mapping the effects of 110Hz. Although it could not be completed quite in time for inclusion in this book, it will be published in another context at a later date.) Anyone interested in finding out more about ICRL should visit their website: http://www.icrl.org.

Charla Devereux and Brenda Dunne suffered the rigours of acoustic fieldwork in Britain and Ireland with Robert Jahn and myself. Both he and I are grateful to them for their invaluable assistance. I also wish to acknowledge Charla's observation concerning the acoustic effect in the Treasury of Atreus tholos tomb at Mycenae, Greece. I thank my son, Sol Devereux, who helped me conduct acoustic fieldwork in Mexico, and who was skilful enough to make digital audio recordings of some elusive echoes.

Special mention must be made of Christopher Chippindale, who encouraged the earlier, tentative explorations of a handful of acoustic archaeological investigators, including this one, during his editorship of *Antiquity*.

There are many people who have supplied me with information and suggestions over what is now several years of acoustic interest in ancient sites on my part, and I would risk accidentally missing out some names were I to attempt to thank them all individually, so I trust they will accept a global "thank you". I must single out Wayne Van Kirk, though, for initially bringing much of the Mayan material to my attention.

This book came about largely because of the timely and rigorous efforts of Stuart Booth, who acted as my agent and also project-managed the operation. My appreciation goes to him. Everyone involved in the Vega imprint at Chrysalis Books should also be commended for their sterling efforts in processing and publishing this work at such terrifyingly short notice.

I thank Rosie Allsop at Third Eye Media and also Sandy Holton at Channel 4 for so helpfully mediating on matters associated with the book's publication. I am most appreciative of Dan Chambers for commissioning the programme on acoustic archaeology for Channel 4 – without that spur this book would doubtless have taken a long time to see the light of day. And a big "thank you" goes to Tony Edwards of Third Eye Media for his unfailing encouragement and general all-round congeniality.

ILLUSTRATIONS

Photographs not sourced by the author are credited in their captions. Credits for figures are also given in their captions as appropriate.

< 6 >

Foreword

Archaeologists study past human lives by the evidence of the material remains; and the material that remains very much directs the kind of story we can tell.

For some regions and periods, it is as if ancient people died without ever having lived: we have burials or cemeteries, but little or nothing to tell of the many years of those lives before they became deaths. If people were buried with grave-goods, we can try to learn from the objects. But what if the objects were special things made largely or only for the grave, like the little devices pushed in or under the corpse by which undertakers today – for all that you or I know – stop our jaws flopping open in the coffin, or our whole bodies sliding to the foot end with a thump if the bearers tip the box? Those artefacts, if they exist, would be conspicuous in any account of the twenty-first century that was made from the material evidence of our cemeteries – unknown though their existence is to you or me.

Accordingly, the story we archaeologists can tell is always selective, and one way it is selected is in its bias amongst the senses. Sight and feel are there, for many material objects that ancient people saw and felt do survive. Even so, they are slanted. The overall colour of a prehistory museum gallery is grey, beige, and brown, for it is objects in durable materials of those dull colours that survive – starting with dull stone and dull pottery. Even the bright objects have been dulled: the ancient bronze axe that once flashed yellow we see today corroded to a sombre, dirty, dark green. Silver turns dark purple or black. Only gold stays pure in the ground, and glistens just as it did in ancient lives.

One sense that perishes almost completely is smell. One of my own first archaeological experiences was smelly, and I can still remember –

with thanks – the smell of it. It was in the English medieval tower at Ludgershall, in north Wiltshire, where Peter Addyman was digging the castle, and I as a schoolchild novice was trying to begin to learn the business. We were digging out the deposits from a latrine, wheelbarrow-full after wheelbarrow-full. It was satisfying to dig through with a shovel, not heavy, without either stones or grit. And it was colourful, brown understandably, but brown with a good dash of yellow in the tone, and scattered with many striking specks of other and varied strong colours, for all the world like a congealed mass of ancient vomit, perhaps lightly mixed with some beaten egg.

Did the medieval people of Ludgershall Castle really have such runny tummies? Had they really been eating all diced carrots and green peppers and red peppers? (No, not peppers; peppers come from the Americas, and all Ludgershall is well before 1492.) Then there was the matching smell. It was gentle, unmistakable and sustained, becoming stronger in the afternoon, as the air temperature rose and as fresh medieval deposits were disturbed, as young people energetically shoveling in a confined space added their own scent. And all of it lingering like the heavy odour of rotting garbage on us and on our clothes afterwards.

With all our plumbing, and hygiene, and daily showers, and clean clothes every single day, and all those deodorants and air-fresheners, and food that is excessively clean and pure and sterilized and refrigerated, our modern experience of human smell is reduced and restricted. At the same time our experience of another sense, sound, is also profoundly transformed. Most of us, in the towns where the majority of us live – but even in the English countryside – inhabit a noisy world of modern and artificial sounds.

Once, recording a radio programme with Paul Devereux on Dragon Hill by the Uffington White Horse, in the calm of rural Oxfordshire, I remember how often we had to break off our conversation as the country peace, which the producer wanted as background to our talking together

< 8 >

about that ancient place, was overlain with modern sounds. When it was not jets above us, as the morning transatlantic flights outward-bound from Heathrow climbed to cruising altitude, it was trains below us, speeding through the Vale of the White Horse on the main westbound line out of London's Paddington station; and when it was neither, it was a car labouring past and up to the White Horse car park.

Few of us now know the quiet country sounds. Instead, we choose noise: we turn the radio on to fill the silence; we expect background music in the hotel lobby or the shopping mall; we must have good sounds vibrating in the car as well as the engine, the tyres, the rush of air. Even fewer of us, sleeping without the shuttering wall of a building, know what it is like to hear the eerie night-time calls, which travel for mile upon mile over the ridges and through the stillness, of an Australian dingo, or of a European or Canadian wolf.

Consequently, we are unlikely ever to experience, even for a few days and nights, anything like that other world of sound that ancient people experienced; or to know how those sounds of the dingo or the wolf – or the sudden sight of a great owl dropping down and gliding low by the camp fire – shake your mind in the still of the night. That is why, without that direct experience, so few of us know why it might be that dingoes, wolves and owls have been given so large a place in ancient peoples' worlds and stories.

What was sound like in ancient and prehistoric times? The world was quieter, so its natural sounds – the growing roar of a waterfall first heard a mile or more away and slowly growing to fill and shake the air when you are right under it; the shriek of a thousand grasshoppers in an Alpine summer meadow; the thump, crash and whirr when a grouse or a capercaillie jumped out from under your very feet and flew beating up; the varied movements and sounds a dying animal makes when you the hunter or farmer have killed it – were all stronger, far more so than what we now experience of the same sounds, but within the insulated artificial noise of a car.

< 9 >

We can suppose the human sounds that filled that quieter world were more intense too, and human sounds were more intensely experienced. If you did not sing or chant or make music or rhythm yourself, there would be no sound of singing or chanting or of music or of rhythm.

We know that is the case, because the artificial world of noise is very much a making of our own time and culture, invented first by the machinery of the industrial age, then by the twentieth-century electric culture of mass-communications. In the European culture of our great-grandparents' time, and of their great-grandparents', and in the indigenous cultures of the whole world that Europeans encountered (and largely washed away in recent centuries), we know there was a different experience of sound. It was an experience we can reasonably think was the common experience of all humankind save that small number of us who instead live as Westerners in modern times.

So there needs to be an "archaeology of sound", an archaeology of sound which is made – like all archaeologies – from the material evidence. This pioneering study by Paul Devereux explores the archaeology of sound, and makes the first considered sketch of the human experience it contains. (And it really is pioneering: when I search 1,387,529,000 web pages through google.com on the Internet for "Archaeology Sound", the search engine produces nothing about it anywhere).

Of course, any one of us can make sound today at an ancient place or archaeological site: deep caves are especially good, and it takes only six or eight people going "Oummmm" together rhythmically to get a wonderful sensory sound going. Any rock-shelter will do. I recommend particularly, from experience, the Hypogeum in Malta, that singular Neolithic site which was cut as an artificial complex chamber down into soft globigerina limestone and filled with the bones of thousands upon thousands of ancient people. Any ancient place can be filled with sound, and any ancient place can seem different to us because of the sound – witness the people who go to Stonehenge at midsummer and

< 10 >

chant and sing and bang gongs and recite and blow horns, and feel the meaning of the place that way.

So it needs something more systematic: not just "Here is an ancient place where you can make sounds, and be thrilled or moved by them", but "Here is an ancient place whose structure and order and size and shape and controlling human logic are such that we can reasonably conclude sounds were part of its ancient purpose and use and meaning, as evident in the care taken to create it that way."

Like all archaeological enquiries, it will fall short of absolute proof, but it can reach reasonable probabilities. It will benefit from our knowledge of what human societies commonly do, from how consistently they use dance and rhythm and rhythmic repetition. In addition, as many aspects of archaeology are beginning to do, it will benefit from our increasing knowledge of how human minds and brains work. It will assist understanding of the biochemical and physiological reasons that lie behind why dance and rhythm and rhythmic repetition are so powerful as human experiences. And it will also show us why human cultures, in all times and places, have made sound, and why the things which sound leads to were central to their human lives.

Christopher Chippindale
Cambridge University Museum of Archaeology & Anthropology

< 11 >

Introduction

People in remote antiquity would probably have heard with greater acuity than we do, living as they did in a quieter world, a world in which listening for danger would have been a constant and more important activity than in modern times. In such an environment of carefully heard natural sounds it is inconceivable that ancient people would have selected a cave or built a monument in which the acoustics were not absolutely right for whatever ritual activity was to be carried out there. Yet we have tended to be deaf to this likelihood, and when we visit megalithic monuments or ruined temples our preconceived pictures of the past run like silent movies in our heads.

Ancient people had ears as well as eyes, and they would have lived in a world of sound: the classical temples of the Mediterranean world would have resounded to singing and musical instruments; the gaunt stone circles out on the moors of northern Europe would have echoed to the commanding voices of druid-like priests; and the painted caves of the Old Stone Age, as well as the megalithic chambers inside the New Stone Age mounds of the dead, would have resonated to the chanting and drumming of shamans or reverberated with deeply intoned oracular pronouncements.

Archaeological investigators are just beginning to remedy their "time deafness", and are starting to undertake various types of acoustical enquiry. As a consequence, tentative new evidence is beginning to emerge of how people used prehistoric sites. This book tells the story of this embryonic movement in archaeology, in the course of which will be described the uses of sound in the ancient world for trance-induction and for oracular purposes, as well as for ritual and celebratory functions.

The study of sound can be presented in highly technical ways –

sometimes almost distressingly so for non-acousticians – but because the use of sound in archaeological and ethnological contexts is a matter of the soul as much as of the science, and as this book is intended for general readers, I have minimized technical content as far as possible, while providing references to more technical sources for those who wish to pursue those aspects further.

The juxtaposition of living sound and ancient, long-dead sites conjures up notions of us being allowed to listen in on the past. While this is overly romantic, it does contain just a germ of truth.

Paul Devereux
Cotswolds, England

< 13 >

PART ONE

The Sounds of Time

Sound in the ancient world was conceived of as a supernatural phenomenon. This section of the book overviews the mysticism, history and anthropology of sound in order to remind ourselves what our ancestors thought about it – beliefs unfamiliar to a modern, Western audience, but which still persist in some traditional cultures. The wonder with which the ancient mind treated the magic of sound provides a necessary backdrop against which the modern acoustical explorations of ancient sacred places described in Part Two can best be appreciated. If we think of sound only in the modern way, as a relatively inconsequential effect, we risk missing the significance of the new acoustical findings that are being made in archaeology today. This section also charts acoustical effects on the mind and body, showing that there is more to sound than meets the ear. The archaic approach to sound might still have things to teach us.

CHAPTER ONE:

Spirits and Sound

How people once thought of sound was very different from our automatic understanding of it today as being due to pressure waves vibrating in the air (or some other medium). Instead, strange noises and echoes would have been associated by ancient peoples with spirits and the non-physical otherworld.

ANCIENT ECHOES

Emerging in the last centuries BC, ancient Greece can be viewed as a kind of cross-over culture, straddling the shift between the archaic "dreamtime" past, when sounds were thought of in this spiritual way, and the beginnings of rationalistic thought in which the acoustical properties of structures such as theatres were beginning to be considered (see below).

Examples of how the archaic view lingered in ancient Greece can be found in its mythology, where natural forces were personified as gods. Sound is represented by the figure of Echo, a former nymph. The Greeks told two main myths about her: in one, she fled the advances of Pan, the nature god, who took his revenge by sending madness upon some shepherds who tore her to pieces, leaving only her voice; and in the other, her chattering so irritated the goddess Hera that she was consequently deprived of all speech except for being able to repeat the last word anyone spoke to her. In this condition, Echo tried to seduce Narcissus, but after being rejected by him she wasted away until nothing was left but her voice – one that could repeat only what anyone said in its vicinity.

VOICES OF THE GODS

A less obvious example of the continuation of a spiritual approach to sound in ancient Greece is the enthusiastic recourse its people made to oracle sites – a phenomenon found elsewhere in the late prehistoric Mediterranean world. Oracles were places where the voices of the gods could be made manifest in answer to questions posed by mortals, and many such locations were reputed to issue sounds in one way or another.[1] Most oracles had – or came to have – resident priests or priestesses who conducted the oracular interpretation, but some also "spoke" directly to the inquirer. For example, the oracle site at Dodona, whose ruins today stand near the foot of Mount Tomaros, was one of the oldest and most important of all. There it was claimed that Zeus spoke through a sacred and "voiceful" oak tree, although it would seem that it was the rustling sound made by wind blowing through the tree's foliage that was the god's "voice". Another audible effect at Dodona was a "sounding brass", a cauldron that was made to reverberate, and the ensuing sound was then interpreted. One description of how this was done explains that a statue was placed next to the cauldron, and when the wind disturbed chains that were attached to the statue, the metal struck the brass vessel and caused it to vibrate. A third form of acoustic divination at Dodona was by the interpretation of the murmurings of a spring or fountain there. The oracle of Trophonius, on the side of a mountain at Lebedeia, not far from Delphi, was the location of another "direct" oracle, set amid soaring precipices and rocky ravines. Before descending to the oracle itself, the suppliant prepared by spending a number of days eating a special diet and undergoing cleansing rituals. At the appropriate time, attendant priests would lead the petitioner at night down to a river, where he or she bathed and was anointed with oil; then they were taken to two fountains, called "forgetfulness" and "memory", and given draughts prepared from their waters (drinks that may have contained mind-altering herbs). The visitor would then pray and make offerings before a secret statue of Trophonius, and finally

< 18 >

they would proceed to an enclosure which contained an artificially constructed "chasm in the earth", as described by the second-century AD Greek writer and traveller Pausanias. Entering this, the inquirer went down a ladder and then had to struggle feet first through a fairly small hole, whereupon they slipped rapidly down to a cavern and shrine. The suppliant learned of the future "sometimes by sight and at other times by hearing" states Pausanias, somewhat enigmatically. One suggestion has been that the "voice" of Trophonius was a roaring underground stream or flume. A similar situation existed at a chasm in Boetia, north of the Gulf of Corinth, where Amphiaraus, a heroic prince of Argos, was said to have been pushed to his death by an angry Zeus. His "voice" was heard for centuries afterwards answering queries put to him by visitors. The Greeks also flocked to Egypt to visit two statues, 18 metres (60 feet) tall, which they called the Colossi of Memnon, in the Valley of the Kings near modern-day Luxor (see Plate 1). Now badly eroded, these originally depicted King Amenhotep III and flanked the entrance to his mortuary temple, which no longer survives. After an earthquake in 27BC, the northernmost statue was severely cracked and began to emit strange sounds at sunrise – perhaps due to heat expansion as the sun warmed up the stone. Its sounds were said to range from the crackle of a cord snapping to the more melodious tone of a musical note. The Greeks took the sounds to be the utterings of Memnon, the mythical African hero whose father Tithonos had shrunk with great age until he was little more than a voice.

SPIRIT PLACES

When the age of oracles came to a close in the early centuries AD, the idea of sounds being spiritual manifestations gradually passed out of mainstream Western culture. However, in tribal societies anthropologists still find spiritual connotations being attributed to sound. So, for example, the French anthropologist Lucien Levy-Bruhl noticed that the Marind-anim people of Papua New Guinea identified certain places

< 19 >

– chasms, river channels and swamps – as the abodes of *dema*, or spirits, because "curious noises may be heard in them".[2] Similarly, in the country of the Wintu Indians of northern California a spirit residing in a cave, spring or river feature is said to often make its presence known "through an audible buzzing".[3] Ninaistakis, the sacred mountain of the Blackfoot people of Montana, was revered and formed the centre of ancient vision-questing practice not only because it is prominent and looks like a chief's headdress, but also because it "sings". This emission of sound is created by the ever-present wind blowing through the erosion-formed ridges, spires, cracks and crevices on its summit. Archaeologist Brian Reeves refers to it as a veritable "sound system". It is apparent that the association of unusual sounds with the presence of spirits was quite universal.

SPIRITS IN THE ROCKS

Some ancient cultures believed that spirits existed in rocks, or beyond and behind the rock surface. Echoes reflect from rock-faces, and the sounds were once almost certainly taken as being spirits issuing from beyond the veil of the rock-surface. It is ironic that the realization of the likelihood of this prehistoric explanation for echoes developed because of a visual factor – namely, rock-art. In the last two decades of the twentieth century, some archaeologists began to suspect that the rock surface on which prehistoric rock-imagery was painted or engraved was not just an artist's "blackboard" on which signs were scrawled, but may have had a significance of its own. Two of the first people to propose this were David Lewis-Williams and Thomas Dowson of Witwatersrand University in Johannesburg. They were studying ancient San or Bushman rock-art and noticed that some paintings were depicted as entering or leaving the rock-face. They had already assembled powerful ethnological evidence that the rock-art painters were shamans (see box opposite). When shamans go into trance, they often visit the spirit world via a "tunnel", a common hallucinatory feature experienced by

< 20 >

Shamanism

Shamanism is a magico-religious practice known in tribal societies worldwide, and even in more stratified societies where the shamanic role developed into a theocratic structure. The origins of shamanism are thought to date back 20–40,000 years. The shaman acts as a healer, psychologist, diviner, conjuror, sorcerer and knowledge-holder, all combined. Their defining characteristic is the ability to voluntarily enter trance in order to have an ecstatic (out-of-body) experience in which the soul can travel to the spirit-realms – the otherworlds of gods, ancestors and elemental powers – in order to, variously, obtain information and supernatural powers, to guide the souls of dying tribal members into the afterworld, or to fight demons or enemy shamans. This "shaman's journey" is most often experienced as an aerial flight – and shamanic imagery is rich with bird-related symbolism which expresses this – but it can also be pictured as a spirit-journey through the physical landscape. Trance states are traditionally achieved by means of drumming or other forms of repetitive percussion, but alternate methods (often combined) include chanting, dancing, fasting, sleep and sensory deprivation, and the use of mind-altering plant substances. Shamans have the ability to not only readily enter trance, but also to emerge from it voluntarily, and to retain full memory of what they saw or heard while in the "otherworld".

While shamanism may be thought of today as a primitive religious expression, the great antiquity of the practice means that shamans can, in fact, possess a deep and sophisticated understanding of the human mind, knowledge that is comparable to the way that shamans in rainforest environments tend to possess much greater information about botanical sources of medicines than exists in modern science.

< 21 >

people of any place or time in all kinds of trance, whether ritual- or drug-induced or resulting from a near-death experience. The South African researchers suspected this "tunnel" sometimes started at the walls of rock-shelters.

"Shaman-artists depicted some of the visions they brought back from the spirit world as if they were emerging from the rock face," Lewis-Williams and Dowson observed.[4] One visual feature they noted recurring in the rock-art was a red line fringed with white dots: as just one example, a line like this linked the image of an antelope to small grooves and steps in the surface of the rock. Frequently, rock-art panels depict a person or animal walking along sections of such a line before it enters a tiny crack or crevice, only for it to reappear a few centimetres further along. In other cases, creatures seem to disappear into or emerge from cracks in the rock – an example in eastern Orange Free State shows a set of antelope heads emerging from a fissure. Rock-art serpents in particular are often depicted as slithering into or out of cracks. In some examples, creatures are depicted as though parts of them are obscured behind the rock face.

Another characteristic of people undergoing trance is that they feel as if their body image changes – it can seemingly transform into that of an animal (usually a symbolic totemic or power creature in the relevant tribal religious contexts), or it can become distorted or change size. To this day, the San of the Kalahari say they can become "very small" when they enter trance states during their dances. It would have been in such altered visionary forms that the shaman would have entered the cracks and crevices in the rock surfaces of his ritual cave, rock-shelter or outcrop.

As with the notion that unusual sounds were associated with spirits, the idea of the spirit world existing behind rock faces seems to have been fairly universal. Lewis-Williams and the French rock-art expert Jean Clottes think this is evident in the Palaeolithic caves of western Europe. They note that many images incorporate features of the surface

< 22 >

on which they were placed. Sometimes a natural undulation in the rock is incorporated into the painting of a bison or other creature thereby giving a three-dimensional form to its body, from a shoulder or chest to an eye. Similarly, the edge of a rock-shelf has been used to delineate the line of a creature's belly or backbone. Again, the painted animals of the Palaeolithic caves seem to appear out of the rock's surface: for example, at Rouffignac in France's Dordogne region, a horse's head is painted on the side of a protruding flint nodule, implying that the rest of the horse is behind the rock face. The archaeologists also noted another intriguing aspect of this same phenomenon – the use of shadows. When a lamp or flaming torch is placed in certain positions, the shadows cast across the rock walls sometimes suggest the shape of part of an animal. "Then only a few deft strokes were needed to add the head, legs, and belly," Lewis-Williams and Clottes remark.[5] If the light source is moved, the shadows flee and the animal, in effect, disappears back through the rock surface. The researchers feel that the cave walls and ceilings were but a "thin 'membrane'" standing between the people who ventured into the depths of the cave and the spirit world behind its surfaces. Entranced shamans or vision-questers sought to enter this world through orifices in the rocks, or to draw out spirit (power) animals from beyond the rocky veil. Such animals would, of course, have been visions or hallucinations caused by mind-altered states, and scientific research has shown that when such hallucinations are experienced with open eyes the imagery appears to be projected onto the surroundings.[6] It is also the case that when in a mind-altered state a person's perceptions become much more acute, so the swellings, depressions and flaws in rock-surfaces would have been more noticeable than during the normal state of consciousness.

In the United States, archaeologist David Whitley has observed in ancient Native American rock-art a similar interaction with the intricacies of rock surfaces. A classic example occurs at a site known as McCoy Spring near Blythe in southern California. A broken boulder at

< 23 >

the site has the carving of a stick-like human figure turning into a wiggly line that links to one of the pronounced cracks in the boulder (see Plate 2). From his ethnological research, Whitley deduces this to be the depiction of a rattlesnake-shaman and his spirit-helper, the snake. The imagery portrays the shaman "transforming back into a person from his supernatural alter ego, the snake, as he emerges from a crack – a portal to the sacred realm – in the rock face".[7] Rock-art sites in this vast region are referred to in local dialects as places "to go under", "to drown", "to be lifted up" – all metaphors for the sensations experienced in trance states, with "to go under" specifically referring to the penetration of the hidden spirit world through the "veil" formed by the surface of the ground or a rock-face.

It is not just developed rock-art imagery that marks a rock face as sacred: sometimes daubs of pure pigment convey the fact. In some of the South African examples, red paint was applied around hollows or steps in the rock-surfaces and black pigment along grooves or folds. This is similar to Canada where, in Sakatchewan, Manitoba and Ontario, there are cliffs that are painted simply with a red ochre wash. This marks them as special places, places where "dreams" (trances) were had and where *manitous*, or spirits, were believed to live. (It may well be that these places also produce strong echoes, thereby compounding the overwhelming sense of spirit-power that would be felt by visitors to the site.) In Ontario, gifted shamans were said to have had the power to enter the rocks, meet the *manitous* residing beyond the cliff-face and exchange tobacco for "medicine" (supernatural power).[8]

Such widely found ideas about rock-art and the existence of a spirit world beyond the rock surfaces undoubtedly paralleled the equally widespread belief that echoes were the voices of spirits living in rocks and cliffs, sounds that emanated from rock surfaces that were especially holy. In considering the ancient significance of sound, then, it is crucial for us to appreciate the supernatural context in which it was understood to occur.

< 24 >

CHAPTER TWO

Cultural Perspectives

We can too readily overlook the fact that not all cultures were as dominated by the visual sense as is the modern, Western one. Some peoples placed much trust in the ear and hearing was as important, if not more so, than seeing – yet to most people today, seeing is believing. "Most of our thinking is done in term of *visual* models, even when an auditory one might prove more efficient," observed Edmund Carpenter and Marshall McLuhan in a perceptive essay in which they drew attention to our cultural deafness to acoustic space.[9] We can take two profoundly dissimilar traditional cultures, one in the Arctic and the other in a tropical rainforest, to illustrate attitudes to sound which are markedly different to our own.

ARCTIC ACOUSTICS

Edmund Carpenter studied the people known as Eskimos. The traditional Eskimo habitation is dome-shaped – winter snow igloos and summer sealskin tents. Carpenter noted that within an igloo there are no flat, static walls to arrest the ear or eye, "but voices and laughter come from several directions".[10] The same is true of the sealskin tent – "Every sound outside can be heard within, and women always seem to be turning and stretching so they can peer out through holes in the tent … They define space more by sound than sight," Carpenter states. In Eskimo culture, oral tradition is so strong as to make the eye subservient to the ear – truth is given through oral tradition. "To them, the ocularly visible apparition is not nearly as common as the purely auditory one; *hearer* would be a better term than *seer* for their holy men," says Carpenter.[11]

SOUNDS OF THE FOREST

Anthropologist Alfred Gell studied in a very different environment – the rainforests of Papua New Guinea. Gell conducted fieldwork with the Umeda people in 1969–70, but a long time afterwards he realized that that there was much about his study that he would want to strongly revise, because he understood that he had approached the Umeda in a characteristically Western visual way, rather than by paying proper attention to the acoustic dimension of their culture, and by so doing he had missed much of its essence.[12] During his fieldwork Gell had become frustrated at not being able to obtain "views" of anything – he never saw a complete native village, for example. For fourteen months his sight was limited to tens of metres – half a kilometre at most. He now knew, as more recent anthropological studies have begun to reveal, that the intimate, "vibrant, tactile, scented gloom" of the forest peoples' environment made hearing the prime sense, not sight. Indeed, sight came only third in the sensory pecking order after hearing and smell. To really understand these people and their world-view, one had to enter their "auditory domain", as Gell puts it.

This difficulty for visually dominated Westerners is well expressed in an incident that Gell had when living with the Umeda people. It was dusk and a Umeda man burst into the anthropologist's hut in a panic-stricken state. He had just had a frightening experience on a forest path leading to the village. He had been chased by a *yawt*, a forest ogre believed in by all Umeda. The man had heard the *yawt* panting "hu-hu-hu" in the darkness among the trees alongside the path; suddenly it circled round and confronted the poor fellow, still going "hu-hu-hu". The man was forced to cut through the forest to avoid the monster. "Yes, yes – but did you actually see the ogre?" Gell wanted to know. His informant was perplexed. "It was dark, I was running away, it was there on the path going 'hu-hu-hu'," he repeated with exasperation. For Gell, and Westerners in general, the *yawt* could be real only if it was seen, but for the Umeda the primary sense was hearing and that was the determinant of reality.

< 26 >

Cultural Perspectives

BIRDSONG

The Kaluli are another tribal people from Papua New Guinea, and they consider the birdsong emanating from the dense foliage around them to be the voices of the dead, or, more accurately, they believe the living birds embody the spirit voices. Bird classification is based not on what birds look like, but on the kind of songs they have. But birdsong is only one kind of "acoustic coding of the environment" used by the Kaluli, according to Gell. The sounds produced by rivers, streams and waterfalls has also entered their language and poetics.[13] "The descending movement of Kaluli song is the sung equivalent of a waterfall, and particular streams and falls are perpetually evoked in the texts of Kaluli songs..." Gell writes. "Place, sound and social memory are fused together in Kaluli poetics."

When discovering acoustic effects in the ruined structures of rainforest people such as the ancient Maya, as we do in Chapter 10, it is particularly important for us to bear in mind the special power that sound had in such cultures – and perhaps for many other societies in the prehistoric past.

SUPERNATURAL SOURCES OF SOUND

What people think about the origins of music can also differ widely from culture to culture. Modern Westerners know to their satisfaction that music is a non-mysterious phenomenon resulting from specially crafted instruments and human skill in manipulating the voice, and that it probably began tens of thousands of years ago with bone whistles and developed over the intervening ages into what can be appreciated today. But people in other societies have different ideas, and these ideas can determine the function and performance of music.

In Africa, the Asaba people of Nigeria are of the opinion that every fresh dance or song was first heard by hunters during their expeditions in the jungle and can be attributed to forest spirits. Myth has it that music was first brought to the Asaba by a legendary hunter called

< 27 >

Orgardie. One day, deep in the jungle, he heard music; hiding himself, he saw it was coming from an approaching group of forest spirits. He watched them long enough to learn their songs and dances, and he brought this knowledge back with him to his village. Nigeria's Ibo people, on the other hand, believe that some of their music is a true reproduction of the voices of their ancestral spirits.

Cultural concepts about music are just as rich and varied in Australia and Oceania. In the Solomon Islands, pan-pipes are said to have been invented by the spirits of still-born children, who now live in the hills or in deep holes in the forest. One such child-spirit was captured by humans and the pan-pipes were seized. The Yirkalla Aborigines of Arnhem Land, Australia, considered the burbling of babies to be "revelations of secret and sacred songwords" and used such sounds as the basis of some of their music.[14]

It is by no means only the Kaluli who consider birdsong to be spirit-related. Yakut shamans of Siberia are remarkable for their imitation of bird calls, sounds that appear to have come from disembodied birds flying around inside the shaman's reverberant conical tent. Early anthropologists particularly noted the "calls" of the lapwing, falcon, woodcock, eagle, and, above all, the cuckoo – an especially important spirit-familiar of Yakut shamans. When the shaman's voice broke into a falsetto, it meant that a supernatural spirit-voice or bird was speaking through him. (Interestingly, the Germanic term for magic formula, *galdr*, is related to the verb *galan*, to sing, and is usually applied to birdsong.)

Many cultures used music only in a sacred context. It had no role, or only a carefully circumscribed one, in the mundane, everyday world and was considered too powerful for profane usage. In ancient China and India – and even in Pythagorean Greece (sixth century BC) – music remained closely related to cosmic magic. Music and sound were not to be trifled with.

< 28 >

CHAPTER THREE

Ritual and Sound

Sound – both musical and non-musical – has always been a vital component of most rituals, whether for initiatory, magical, religious, or ceremonial purposes: the commanding or petitioning voice of the celebrant, the singing of congregations and choirs, the chanting of participants, the whistling, clapping, drumming and other percussive sounds made by ritualists, and the use of musical instruments. Sound can define the phases of a ritual, create appropriate moods, signal events and transitions, provide contrast with periods of deliberate silence, enable the ritualist to contact the spirit world, and it can, of course, move the mind and soul emotionally. Anthropologists have noted that while blind ritual specialists are not uncommon, deaf ones are rare.[15] Rituals are often conducted in dim or flickering lighting, or even at night, which in itself causes participants to be more sensitive to the auditory aspects of a ritual (and do we not tend to close our eyes when listening to the music at an orchestral concert?) Anthropologist Donald Tuzin has gone so far as to claim that "the aural is the privileged mode in ritual sensitivity",[16] and it is true that the literature about the ancient world tells us that "voices and noises" were involved in initiation ceremonies.[17]

CAUSING A COMMOTION

Non-musical ritual sounds have taken numerous and sometimes exceedingly bizarre forms. Loud reports, banging, ringing and other kinds of unpatterned sounds have been used in ceremonial, ritual and magical contexts in many cultures down the ages. In Europe noise-making was once customary at times of solar eclipses. This doubtless arose from the belief that the evil entity "eating" the sun could be driven away by the din, because noise-making was widely considered to be effective in deterring demons in many situations. Centuries ago, in England, the custom of "apple-wassailing" or "apple-howling" took place over the Christmas period to ensure a plentiful crop of the fruit. People would beat upon kettles and pans, blow horns, and shout and sing in order to rouse the sleeping tree-spirits and drive off the demons of ill-luck; in later days, men fired guns through the topmost branches of the trees. In Sweden and elsewhere, firecrackers were let off at midnight on Easter Saturday. In many places church bells were used to make what religious historian Mircea Eliade called "the anti-demonic magic of noise" – they would be rung in thunderstorms for example, to protect against lightning, or during plagues to drive off the "demons of disease". As the antiquarian John Aubrey wrote in the seventeenth century: "The curious do say that the ringing of bells exceedingly disturbs spirits." Noise-making to ward off evil spirits went back, of course, to pre-Christian times when making a din in the fields was thought to protect the crops.

STRANGE WORDS OF POWER

The human voice could be used for making strange sounds that were neither musical nor language. The Great Magical Papyrus in Paris tells us that in late antiquity magician-shamans would make weird sounds – clucking, sighing, groaning, smacking of lips, taking a deep breath and releasing it with a hiss.[18] And there were special words: Egyptian inscriptions and papyri tell of "words of power", *hekau*, used in ritual contexts. These were especially important to know at the time of death, and it was even more important for the deceased to be able to enunciate them on entering the otherworld realm, so a key ritual involved with the magical "opening of the mouth" was performed on the completed mummy (Figure 1). As if to emphasize the importance

< 30 >

Fig. 1. The ancient Egyptian "opening of the mouth" ceremony

of sound in Egyptian ritual, on the axial solar alignment that runs through the great temple complex of Karnak, Luxor, there is the "Temple of the Hearing Ear" dedicated to Re-Horakhty, the sun god of the horizon. The importance of special words (usually names) in the ancient Egyptians' magic and religion goes back to their creation myths, in which the creator god, Neb-er-tcher (Khephri, one of the aspects of the sun god Re), brought the cosmos into existence by uttering his own name as a word of power. The same essential myth is found in the Old Testament's "in the beginning was the Word", while the Hebrew YHWH

< 31 >

(Yahweh) represented the name of God, which could not be spoken. To this day it is axiomatic in ritual magical practice that there are words carrying special powers. All such clues resonate with the perceived importance of vocal sound, as it has been used in ritualistic circumstances since remotest antiquity.

WHISTLING UP A VISION

Human whistling also has its place in ritual. It survives today in association with mind-altering substances taken in a ritualistic context. In 1968, anthropologists Fred Katz and Marlene Dobkin de Rios attended healing sessions conducted by shamans with groups of clients in jungle clearings on the outskirts of Iquitos, a remote town in the Peruvian Amazon, where they recorded special whistling incantations used in the rituals.[19] The shaman or healer is known as an *ayahuasquero*, because at the outset of a session he gives his clients ayahuasca, a powerful hallucinogenic drink made from a jungle vine and various other plants, and he typically takes some himself. The drug is used primarily as a diagnostic tool: it causes the client to have visions which reveal the cause of his affliction. In native Amazonia, as in so many ancient and traditional cultures, disease is considered to be caused by spirits or sorcerers and, thus exposed, the healer can then deflect or neutralize the malevolent influence. A session would last for about four hours, and the healer, accompanied by an apprentice, began his work shortly after the drug potion had been administered. The circle of clients would go into their drug-induced visionary states, and the healer would begin his whistling and the shaking of a rattle made from the leaves of a plant called schacapa. Whistling is used because it is believed that this is the way in which the spirits of the forest, and of the ayahuasca vine itself, can be invoked.

Figure 2 shows the notation the anthropologists recorded for one session. The melody is non-metrical and pentatonic for the most part, with intermittent grace notes. In part A, the mode consists of the notes

< 32 >

C, D, E, G and A, and the tonic note is C reached by the starting note G. The brackets in part A, line 2, indicate that these notes are very faint and uneven in duration. The whistling is delivered at 148 pulses per minute – 2–3 Hertz (Hz) or cycles per second. Section A1 continues in much the same fashion, and in part B the tonic note C is reached by the starting note E, but the tone G is predominant. Section C is a repeated motif, which is metrical and interspersed between sections B and A1. The bracketed notes in D represent a musical phrase that predominates the section (the actual sound is lower than the written note). The final section, E, is a hexatonic scale. The letters in this section and the coda notation indicate the substructures of the melody.

Such whistling incantations are used only in ayahuasca rituals, and the anthropologists likened their basic role to that of Gregorian chants in Christianity, insofar as the latter, too, are tonal relationships structured so as to evoke spiritual experience. In the case of the *ayahuasquero* whistling, this role is symbiotic with powerful, drug-induced altered states of mind. "Such phenomena as the slowing down or changing of time perception must be related to how music is perceived by the individual under the effects of the powerful alkaloids, harmine and harmaline, present in the ayahuasca potion," the anthropologists point out. "The number of metronomic markings listed … may not, indeed, be perceived as they would in an ordinary state."

In order to observe the whistling from the "inside", so to speak, Dobkin de Rios took ayahuasca herself during a healing session. Visions appeared and moved very quickly, filling her mind's eye with an intricate panorama of primary colours and variegated forms. She sensed that the speed of the visions was related to the tempo of the healer's whistling. The man then slowed the pace of his whistling, and the sudden, dramatic vision of a woman appeared to the anthropologist: if Dobkin de Rios was subject to the belief system ruling the session, this vision would have represented the person responsible for bewitching her. As it was, the anthropologist noted that

< 33 >

< 34 >

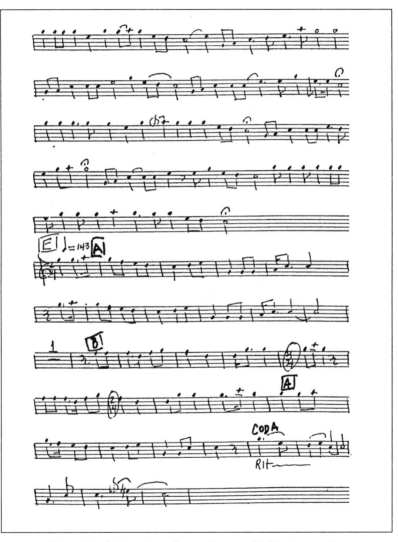

Fig. 2. Musical notation of an ayahuasca whistling incantation.
(F. Katz & M. Dobkin de Rios, 1971)

< 35 >

the appearance of this very real-looking visionary female "could most definitely be related to the velocity of the healer's whistling incantations and the use of his schacapa rattle in rhythmic motions". It became apparent that ayahuasca healers could control the speed of the visions by their whistling and rattling, and the selection of melodies could, moreover, evoke certain types of vision.

As a much more recent pilgrim to Iquitos, the writer and traveller Tahir Shah made similar findings. Under the influence of the drug, Shah had an extraordinarily convincing sensation of being transformed into a giant bird. He would have panicked had it not been for the rattling and whistling incantation ("soft whirring chant") of the shaman, Ramón (see Plate 3). Shah found the shaman's whistle-chant to give a framework to his hallucinatory experience; he could not distinguish the words but they somehow made "perfect sense" because they were "beyond language". The chanting "ordered" him to soar skywards and it felt as if the sound of the schacapa rattle provided his newly found wings with a cushioning of air to assist them. Shah was soon "flying" naturally, and could feel the rush of air on his face. The chanting was like a navigation beacon for the flightpath of the writer's soul.[20]

ALTERING CONSCIOUSNESS

These examples of ritual sounds used by a living traditional culture in the Amazon prompt us to be aware that the acoustic aspects of archaeological sites of former sanctity described in Part Two were probably often intended to augment altered states of consciousness, based on the assumption that ritual activity took place at the sites. This is further underlined by the sensitive observations of Gordon Wasson concerning his experiences on "magic mushrooms" in Mexico. Wasson made news in the 1950s by being one of the very first Westerners to discover that ancient Indian rituals using hallucinogenic mushrooms still survived in a remote village in Oaxaca, Mexico. Scholars up until then had assumed they had died out after the Spanish had arrived centuries before.

< 36 >

Moreover, Wasson and a colleague were the first non-Indians to actually take part in a mushroom ritual – known as a *velada* (vigil). The Mazatec Indian *curandera*, Maria Sabina, gave the participants, including Wasson and his companion, portions of mushrooms, and the Americans lay down as the hallucinogenic fungi took effect. Sabina began her ritual singing, "not loud, but with authority" Wasson noted.

" It is as though you were hearing it with your mind's ear, purged of all
dross ... In the darkness and stillness, that voice hovers through the hut,
coming now from beyond your feet, now at your very ear, now distant,
now actually underneath you, with strange ventriloquistic effect. "[21]

Wasson described Sabina's singing as a "percussive chant" because with her hands she hit her chest, her thighs, her forehead, and her arms – each body part with its own resonance – continually modulating and syncopating the blows so as to produce "a most complicated percussive beat". As with Shah, Wasson noticed that his spirit seemed "to soar... and with the speed of thought to travel where it listeth" in time with the sounds produced by the *curandera*.

THE "JUNGLE GYM"

In later work, Dobkin de Rios and Katz probed further into why the use of sound and vocal music was so integral to traditional drug rituals. They came to the conclusion that the music acted as a link between the worlds of ordinary waking consciousness and the often fearsome worlds of altered mind states, providing "a set of banisters and pathways" to help the ritualist mentally navigate under the influence of whatever sacramental plant hallucinogen was being used. In addition, it provided reassurance and a calming environment to help the ritualist cope with the fear invoked with the sudden deluge of sensations and images from the unconscious mind that the drugs provoke. And, as Dobkin de Rios and Shah had directly observed, the chanting and whistling seemed able to structure the visions that appeared to the mind's eye. Dobkin de Rios and Katz suspected that one of the ways this worked was due to the

< 37 >

SOUNDS/MUSIC USED IN SELECTED TRIBAL HALLUCINOGEN-BASED RITUALS IN THE AMERICAS

SOCIETY	TYPES OF SOUND/MUSIC	PLANT DRUG USED
Amahuaca (Upper Amazon)	chanting	ayahuasca
Cashinahua (southeastern Peruvian Amazon)	chanting, singing	ayahuasca
Chama (Upper Amazon)	songs, hissing, whistling, rattles	ayahuasca, tobacco juice
Culina (Peruvian Amazon)	singing	ayahuasca
Huichol (north-central Mexico)	singing, horns, guitar, trumpet	peyote cactus
Jivaro (eastern Ecuador)	hollow log drums, whistling, singing	ayahuasca, tobacco juice, species of *Datura*
Mestizos (north coast Peru)	whistling, songs, conch shell	san pedro cactus, *Datura*, tobacco
Menomini (northeastern United States)	songs, drumming	peyote cactus
Navajo (southwestern United States)	drums, singing, whistling, rattles	peyote cactus
Sharanahua (Peruvian Amazon)	chanting, singing	ayahuasca
Tenetehara (Brazil)	chanting, rattles, whistling bell, singing	tobacco, cannabis
Tukano (Colombia)	pan-pipes, gourd rattles, tube drum, singing	piptadenia, vilho snuff, ayahuasca
Yanomano (Venezuela, Brazil)	chants, rattle, singing	tobacco, virola

Source: Dobkin De Rios, M., and Katz, F., 1975 (abstracted and modified)

< 38 >

mathematical precision and structure implicit in all music. This fixed structure is imposed on the intoxicated client or patient by the shaman "who controls to some degree his client's visual options within this ritualized use of music".[22] Learned from generations of his predecessors, the self-same data bank that is still teaching Western pharmaceutical experts about plants and medicines, the shaman would have intimate, expert knowledge of the visionary effects of the plant drugs being used, and the music to accompany these substances would have been designed and honed down the generations to interact with them. The researchers referred to this tribal system as "the jungle gym in consciousness".

In their detailed review of music used in known drug rituals in traditional cultures (see box, opposite), the pair noted that a general characteristic appeared to be the frequency of rattling effects, almost always in consort with whistling or singing, or rapid vibratory sounds. The two researchers were aware that synaesthesia – when an experience of a colour, say, can be an auditory as well as a visual perception – was one of the characteristics of drug-induced trance (see also Chapter 5). They felt that the use of music and sound helped promote such "scrambling of sensory modalities". Such multi-mode perceptions were also encouraged by the use of dancing, bright costumes and colouring, and even taste – a common feature of Amazon ayahuasca rituals, for example, is the use of orange-scented water by participants. "In this case, olfactory heightening came from the patient's own mouth and was perceived by him throughout the entire session."[23]

RITUAL SING-SONG

In some tribal societies ritual singing can in itself provoke entranced visionary states of mind without requiring the addition of plant hallucinogens. This became obvious to ethnologist Dale Olsen when studying the Warao Indians of the Orinoco River Delta in Venezuela.[24] During healing rituals, Warao shamans sing; some of them also use a large gourd rattle, but the greater emphasis is placed on the song. It is

< 39 >

this music that is the "shamanic tool" Olsen observed, and it sends the shaman into a trance in which he becomes transformed into the supernatural being he is invoking with the song. Yet this is a deeply meditative trance and not some wild affair involving spirit possession. The supernatural being is the shaman's spirit-helper who lives in his body. Olsen detected two characteristics of Warao ritual songs that he felt were related to the production of the ecstatic trance state in the shaman: "melodic expansion" and "upward drift". Melodic expansion occurs during the most melodic section of a shamanic healing ritual, specifically when the illness-causing spirit is being named. The melodic scheme of such naming sections is based on the approximate interval of a fifth; descending from this fifth the shaman sings the pitches that correspond to 5 4 3 1 (G, F, E-flat, C, when using C as the reference point). The 3 1 relationship always approximates a minor third. The complete melodic scheme includes fragmentation and often corresponds to the ciphers 5 4 3 1 4 3 1 3 1. Often, however, and *only* during an actual healing ceremony, the basic spread of a fifth is extended or expanded to approximate and major sixths, minor and major sevenths, an octave, or a minor ninth. Olsen recorded a song that lasted forty-five minutes in which the shaman began only two phrases at the interval of a fifth above the principal tone. "He immediately began an octave above the principal tone when one of his fellow shamans let forth with the word '*oya'*," Olsen reported. The main shaman reacted to this word in a way that immediately intensified the music "as if the word came from a spirit".

The spirit association was also present with the "upward shift" that Olsen noticed. This is a gradual but continuous microtonal rise in pitch, a property that seems to be quite common in unaccompanied music of a ritual nature. "Among the Warao Indians, the phenomenon pervades the music in which spirit contact is felt," Olsen reported. So, for example, it also occurs in Warao non-shamanic lullabies, but only when the singer is referring to spirits.

< 40 >

R i t u a l   a n d   S o u n d

The great American anthropologist Weston La Barre singled out Tibetan overtone chanting as being one of the most powerful forms of ritual – and indeed shamanistic – vocal activity. Its authentic form as used by monks to invoke cosmic demons was described by La Barre as being in "incredibly virtuoso male coloratura, on the single syllable, *Om*, in prodigiously *basso profundo sostenuto* two octaves below middle C and lower – against which the soloist cantillates or 'double-sings'". This is achieved by use of resonant spaces in the mouth and skull. La Barre justifiably opines that the sound produced is a "multidimensional monotone" providing an experience "so unbelievable ... as to seem hallucinatory".[25] La Barre considered that the singing of shamans represented the very beginnings of music, pointing out that shamans required a special language other than normal everyday speech with which to address the spirits.

BEATING THE DRUM

In addition to vocal sounds used in ritual, there were, of course, sounds produced by musical instruments – most notably the drum, which is the most common of ritual instruments. Along with the human voice, percussion in general is the most common way tribal ritual sounds are produced: instruments can include gongs, bells, rattles, stamping tubes, sticks (struck together), resounding rocks and even parts of the body (see above), but it is the drum that is pre-eminent. The drum is used not only in shamanic rituals, where it is conceived of as the "steed" or "canoe" that takes the shaman's out-of-body spirit into the otherworld realm, but also in many other contexts where communication with spirits is required. In many cultures the drum is thought of as being sacred. It has been widely noted that there are ancient associations between the drum and the dead – some anthropologists say this is because the instrument is a development of the log coffin.

The sounds were not always musical as such, for vocal and instrumental ritual acoustic effects sometimes (even often) overlapped in a curious way

< 41 >

with drums and other instruments being used to mimic voices – inevitably those of the gods or spirits. The Ashanti in Ghana, for example, use their drums in "speech mode" during certain rituals, especially ones invoking the ancestors. Their ritual drums are made of a specific species of cedar believed to be the abode of the spirit Tweneboa Kodua, and the tree is felled only after due ritual. In "speech mode" the drums are beaten so as to simulate spoken words, which is possible because the Ashanti language is a tone language (one that uses variations in pitch to distinguish words which would otherwise sound identical). The semblance of words, phrases and even whole sentences can be produced on the drums. The drummed language is directed at gods, nature spirits, evil spirits, and the earth, or else at a mediumistic priest or the participants in a ritual.

CULT INSTRUMENTS

An even more sophisticated use of instruments for producing supernatural voices and calls exists among the Arapesh people of Papua New Guinea. Ritual sounds invented there by the men's secret cult known as the Tambaran are specifically designed to represent the voices of highly dangerous cult spirits. The instruments involved take three basic forms: drums and slit-gongs; varying sizes and pitches of whistles, pan-pipes, trumpets and flutes; and bullroarers (objects that make an eerie whirring noise when swung rapidly through the air on the end of a length of cord) and giant amplifying pipes made from hollow, open-ended bamboo tubes up to 4 metres (13 feet) long and 7 centimetres (2–3 inches) wide. The drums and slit-gongs are not secret instruments as such, also being used for open tribal ceremonial activities, but they become secret when modified to produce the supernatural voices. So, for example, a slit-gong becomes a secret instrument when it is modified to invoke the spirit of Nambweapa'w, the Cassowary-Mother: the gong is covered by banana leaves, and a bamboo tube is inserted into the now-enclosed resonating chamber. Sharp, explosive shouts are directed down the tube to create a dull booming sound. This is a magnified but otherwise faithful imitation

< 42 >

of the sound cassowaries actually make.[26] The flutes, pan-pipes, trumpets and whistles are always secret cult instruments, and are used to imitate a range of bird calls, because birds are thought to be the companions and messengers of the spirits.

The amplifying tubes and bullroarers are highly secret instruments. The sounds they make are not intended to imitate anything but rather to manifest the actual presence of spirits in the sounds they produce. Donald Tuzin, an anthropologist who has made a special study of the cult, admits that the sounds are so weirdly disturbing that one is "sorely tempted" to agree with this belief. The bullroarers are used alone or in concert to manifest the voice of Lefin, a red-haired spirit dwarf. The device is swung in a repeating complex pattern, and pitch is varied by slight changes in the tension on the cord. The sound is ambiguous, and like an acoustic inkblot text it is possible to hear in it the words *"Ai tembi-tembineiii; Ai tembi-tembineiii"* ("I am a great, great man; I am a great, great man") in the Arapesh language. Tuzin observed that this carried considerable emotional power when heard in the jungle night. But it is the giant amplifying pipes that create the greatest impact. The operator sings into one end of the tube while the other is placed in a large hourglass drum, much like the bamboo tube inserted into the slit-gong, producing a remarkably enhanced and distorted sound. When twenty or thirty of these pipes are used in unison "the effect especially when heard from a distance over the night air, is stunning".[27] Tuzin described the majesty of the sound as creating the powerful impression "of a chillingly immense, almost human *voice*" – it is that of Nggwal, the greatest of the Tambaran spirits.

SILENT SOUND

Everyone in the cult knew that the sound was manufactured through the pipes, yet all were at the same time convinced that this was not an illusion, but the actual manifestation of Nggwal. Tuzin agreed with his tribal hosts that the sound was sufficiently unusual to justify the sensation that something supernatural was actually present. Why

< 43 >

Infrasound

The human ear is able to distinguish sounds between about 16Hz (Hertz, or cycles per second) and around 20,000Hz (or 20kHz). Optimum human hearing is in the range 500–4000 Hz. The term "infrasound" covers all sound below a notional 20Hz, meaning that generally speaking it cannot be consciously heard by humans. It is a secondary "silent sound", produced in nature by agents that are already noisy at normal levels of audibility, such as wind, the sea breaking on the shore, electrical storms, volcanic eruptions and earthquakes, all of which can issue a broad range of sound frequencies, including low ones. Infrasonic waves are very long, allowing them to travel great distances through many different media. Whales communicate with one another by mean of infrasound – sometimes across entire oceans. Other creatures also use it: for example, most elephant communication is infrasonic, with families several miles apart using it to co-ordinate their patterns of group movement (the infrasonic call of an elephant can carry over an area of 30 square kilometres/11 square miles).

Infrasound is also produced by machinery and other manmade sources.

should this conviction be so strong? Tuzin made some notable observations. He suspected that the cause of the supernatural feeling was the presence of infrasound (see box).

Audible sound reaches the primary processing centres of the brain along certain channels that are not used by the "silent sound" of infrasound. Sound is processed in the brain's temporal lobe, as is language and some aspects of memory. Associated brain structures are involved in feeling,

< 44 >

which would include religious ("numinous") sensations and impressions of spookiness. (Indeed, such feelings are often reported by those who suffer temporal lobe epilepsy.) Tuzin cites some evidence to indicate that infrasonic signals can reach the temporal cortex by circuitous means. He argues that such sounds below the conscious threshold and coming through channels other than the normal auditory ones would in effect be an "eerie miming of audible sound" generating a sense of an unidentified presence in the hearer's mind, which in turn could trigger mysterious associations giving rise to religious or numinous experience. The sounds produced by the secret instruments were "onomatopoeic pseudoutterances", Tuzin averred, simulating "voices" just beyond the limit of normal comprehension – like voices heard in dreams.

In Tuzin's view, percussive instruments, and drums in particular, are commonly used in ritual activities because they produce sounds reminiscent of thunder, and thunder was associated with the powerful sky gods in most traditional cultures. But Tuzin feels that there is more than mimicry involved, pointing out that thunderstorms are known to generate infrasonic waves, as do the winds associated with them (typically between 3Hz and 15Hz). Infrasound can still be "heard" from storms 20 kilometres (12 miles) or more away, even though the audible components of their thunder have been washed out by the distance. He argues that the "calm before the storm" feeling is prototypical of the religious experience.

While he is confident that bullroarers and the amplifying tubes of the Tambaran cult do produce infrasound (as probably do gongs and drums), Tuzin further notes that the times of year when the cult's rituals take place are those when distant thunderstorms are most common in the hills to the south of Arapesh territory: at these times their country is "literally bathed in infrasonic waves of very great intensity". He feels that the infrasonic waves generated by the cult's instruments unite with and exploit "the roar of the unheard thunderstorm".[28] Such matters bring us to the consideration of the physical effects of sound, and to some of the possible reasons why it is such a key element in ritual activity.

< 45 >

CHAPTER FOUR

Mind, Body and Sound

Sound is a physical force, and it has effects that can be seen and felt. This was most famously and classically demonstrated by the "Caruso effect": when travelling in Italy at the turn of the nineteenth century, Dr Albert Abrams saw the great tenor Caruso flick a wine glass with his finger to produce a pure tone. The singer then put down the glass, stepped back a short distance and sang the same note, shattering the glass to fragments.

SOUND'S IMPACT ON THE BRAIN

Because sound is a physical force, the human body can be affected by it, and that includes the brain, for it is a physical organ. That, in turn, means the mind, the non-material "ghost in the machine" of the brain, can be affected. The full story of how the human state of mind can be affected by specifically sound in ritual circumstances has not been fully explored as yet by specialists. What research there is remains rather patchy and incomplete, but enough exists for a few indications to be discerned. As will be seen, Tuzin's feeling seems to be justified that in rituals it is sound at infrasonic levels that is particularly interesting.

Why is drumming or percussion used so prevalently in ritual? That was the question asked by Oxford scholar Rodney Needham, who found it associated in many traditional cultures with rituals of transition – rites of passage such as the shift from childhood to adulthood, initiation, marriage, birth, death.[29] Faint memories of such ritual awareness linger still in Western culture, as in the tying of tin cans to the car taking newly-weds off on their honeymoon. The obvious point is that repetitive, rhythmic drumming and other percussive sounds can generate a hypnotic, trance-like state that is suitable for experiencing supernatural worlds or beings, as well as promoting rhythmic dancing, an activity which itself enhances the condition – especially when it is accompanied by flickering firelight. There is no doubt that observations by anthropologists have indicated the association of drumming with distinctly altered states of consciousness. Writing about voodoo in Haiti, Francis Huxley noted: "it is the drummers who largely provoke dissociation [trance]; they are skilful in reading the signs, and by quickening, altering, or breaking their rhythm they can usually force the crisis on those [dancers] who are ready for it."[30] He considered that the drumming, dancing and singing was specifically aimed at causing the dissociation of the waking consciousness from "its organization in the body" as he put it.

AUDITORY AND PHOTIC DRIVING

Huxley's is a general observation, but some investigators have tried to pin down the actual mechanisms involved in the creation of this "dissociation" or trance effect. Research has particularly centred on the phenomenon of auditory driving, by which is meant the ability of percussion and rhythm to "drive" brainwave frequencies, each group of which is associated with differing states or levels of consciousness (see box, page 48). In the early 1960s Andrew Neher published papers in which he reported the effects of drumming on monitored subjects. Neher observed that a single beat of a drum contains many frequencies, but that these are mainly low frequencies. Laboratory experiments showed that drumming did indeed affect the electrical activity of a subject's brain, particularly in the auditory region. Subjects also reported "unusual perceptions".[31]

The effects of the auditory driving experiments were found to be similar to those obtained by photic driving, in which a subject is exposed to a flashing light (stroboscope), so Neher went on to extrapolate from those findings because there were more of them.

< 47 >

Brainwaves

BRAIN RHYTHMS AND ASSOCIATED FREQUENCIES AND MENTAL LEVELS IN ADULTS

BETA RHYTHM • 13–30Hz

This is associated with the normal waking level of consciousness, involving the engagement of attention with the outside world.

ALPHA RHYTHM • 8–13Hz

This pattern of electrical brain activity is associated with an awake but relaxed state of mind – alert composure. This is considered the normal "base rhythm" of the human brain. It is more prevalent in people when their eyes are closed. Some researchers claim that the dominant presence of this rhythm is a necessary precondition for entry into meditative states.

THETA RHYTHM • 4–7Hz

This pattern of electrical activity tends to appear as a person drifts towards drowsiness. It can appear in dreaming states or in the half-waking "hypnogogic" state. Some researchers have associated this rhythm with deep meditation and trance states when accompanied by other frequencies.

DELTA RHYTHM • 4Hz and lower

This is mainly associated with deep sleep. Some researchers have found it also to be linked with "peak" experiences, or higher levels of consciousness.

Note: This is, of course, a simplified listing. In reality different types of brainwave can occur together and can be affected by a great many factors, both internal and external. The rhythms and associated mental levels can also vary between individuals.

< 48 >

These showed that such stimulation can produce a range of subjective phenomena: perception of coloured moving patterns; sensations of swaying, spinning, and vertigo; tingling and prickling feelings; emotional responses ranging from fear to pleasure; disturbance of time sense; and even the production of organized hallucinations of various types. The best frequency range for such responses to light was in the alpha rhythm range, but laboratory results persuaded Neher that slightly lower frequencies would be most effective for sound stimulation "due to the presence of low frequencies (theta rhythms) in the auditory region of the cortex".

Some subsequent studies have supported Neher's view that ritual drumming, especially in shamanic contexts, does tend to "drive" brain rhythms into the low-frequency theta range. For example, in studying ritual drumming among the Salish Indians of America's Northwest Coast region, researchers found that frequencies in that range were indeed produced.[32] Another study was conducted at the University of Munich by Felicitas Goodman in 1983. Four subjects were closely monitored as they entered a trance state, apparently in response to the sound of a rattle or drum. A "steady stream" of theta waves was measured, along with a range of other biological markers: there were lowered levels of stress compounds, such as adrenalin, noradrenalin and cortisol, in the blood, and lowered blood pressure (curiously combined with heightened pulse rate).[33]

Nevertheless, there have also been criticisms by some researchers, who point out that in real life native drumming rituals use a wide variety of rhythms, producing stimuli that constantly vary – as distinct from the constant beats produced in Neher's laboratory. Neher had, in fact, forestalled this criticism by having already pointed out that, because brainwave frequencies can vary from one individual to another, it would be expected that in actual ritual conditions frequencies would vary to accommodate a range of participants. He noted, for example, that this happened quite deliberately in the case of shamanic seances in

< 49 >

Siberian tribes.[34] But the issue of auditory driving is not clear cut, and as it currently stands the research on it does not have the depth of experimental and clinical literature to support it, such as photic driving does. However, fairly recent work (1990) has confirmed that appropriate drumming does indeed begin to increase theta rhythms in native people after about nine minutes, and that it "plateaus" at fifteen minutes.[35] So it does finally look as if auditory driving is likely to be at least one of the ways in which drumming and percussion work in rituals, though current researchers are at pains to emphasize that other factors can come into play too, particularly the setting of the ritual itself, such as the resonance of the space it is taking place within, and the beliefs and expectations of participants.

THE BODY LANGUAGE OF SOUND

While the detailed and subtle effects of sound in general on consciousness are still subject to investigation, some broader effects, both physiological and physical, have been recorded. Most of the human body resonates at low frequencies, as the data in the box opposite shows. It can be seen that the body can resonate at various frequencies depending on what position it is in. It is important to note that this table shows vibration-resonant frequencies, not infrasonic ones as such. Mechanically induced vibration constitutes a different but related field of research, because infrasound itself is, of course, vibration. The similarities between the two are that in low frequencies the inner ear is an important receptor, and vibration and infrasound occur together in many situations. The subjective effects produced can also be similar,[36] but obviously those produced by vibration are likely to be much more marked and even different to the subtler stimulus of infrasound.

INFRASOUND

Although for practical purposes it is assumed that infrasound is below the threshold of hearing (the limit usually being given as

< 50 >

VIBRATION RESONANT FREQUENCIES FOR SELECTED PARTS OF THE HUMAN BODY

These parts of the body or body structures resonate naturally at the following frequencies, and will respond to any such frequencies in the environment around them.

	Hz
WHOLE BODY:	
lying down	2
standing (relaxed)	4–5
sitting	5–6
Head (when seated)	2–8
Head	20–30
Eyeball	40–60
Eardrum	1,000
Main torso	3–5
Thorax	3–5
Chest wall	60
Spinal column	8
Abdominal mass	4–8
Pelvic area (semi-prone)	8
Hip:	
sitting	2–8
standing	4

Source: NASA–STD–3000/Vol1/REV.A (abstracted)

< 51 >

approximately 20Hz[37]), experiments using high-intensity infrasound have shown that there are people who can detect tones down to between 7 and 5Hz, and some can actually pick up tones down to 1Hz.[38] The perception of such tones at these low levels has variously been described by subjects as "a pumping sound", "popping effect", or "chugging noise" – presumably either separate soundwave peaks or harmonics produced by distortions in the ear mechanism rather than the infrasound itself.[39] Below about 5Hz the heartbeat can interfere with the perception of such low frequencies.[40]

Interest in researching the effects on humans of infrasound, and low-frequency (low-pitched) sound in general, increased with the development of modern machinery. An oft-quoted incident is the case of the draughtsmen working in a sound-insulated environment close to the test-bed of the Concorde engines who complained of nausea, dizziness, lethargy and an inability to concentrate. It was found that these effects were due to infrasonic components in the engine noise, proving that such effects did not only occur at high intensities.

Certain specific effects of moderate intensity infrasound have been noted. One is the sensation of dizziness and sensations of motion due to its upsetting the delicate balance mechanisms within the ear (the vestibular apparatus of the inner ear). At between 2 and 5Hz the physical effects on human subjects of infrasound include a pressure build-up in the middle ear; difficulty in swallowing; difficulty in speaking and voice modulation; chest wall vibration; and post-exposure headaches. At 15–20Hz there may be difficulty in speaking and voice modulation; middle ear pain; strong chest, abdominal and nasal cavity vibration; gagging sensations; and watering of the eyes.

PSYCHOLOGICAL EFFECTS

Most technical investigation into infrasound is conducted to test for the impact on operators of machinery or those travelling in vehicles

< 52 >

(ranging from cars to rockets). Such physical effects might not be expected to occur very often in ritual conditions, where sound intensity levels would presumably be lower (though this may not necessarily always be true, depending on the space in which a ritual is taking place and the loudness of the sounds being made). Generally, however, it is subtler ("magical") acoustic effects and psychological, mental reactions that would be considered.

In one test at 15–20Hz all the subjects experienced "sensations of fear", including shivering.[41] Swaying and falling sensations, as already mentioned, were common in the 5–15Hz range. Drowsiness was commonly reported at all frequencies between 5 and 20Hz, as was post-exposure fatigue. Lack of concentration was frequently reported in the 5–15Hz range. It was generally noted during experiments that the psychological effects are more intense when the whole body is being stimulated by infrasound,[42] and that infrasound and alcohol combine to produce effects on task performance that are much greater than either the sound or the substance on its own.[43] One wonders if this would also be the case with hallucinogenic drugs.

SONIC GHOSTS

Research of this kind is generally conducted for safety considerations to determine if harmful effects will occur, so the possible positive, spiritual, mind-altering potential of infrasound tends not to be scrutinized. However, certain experiments showed that some subjects experienced euphoric feelings at "relatively low levels of infrasound".[44] There are also some extraordinary recent indications that infrasonic frequencies can induce highly specific hallucinatory effects. Engineer Vic Tandy has found that in two places where hauntings have been reported, a workshop and a fourteenth-century cellar, these can be explained as having resulted from the neurophysiological effects created in susceptible witnesses by a prevailing low-frequency sound in the environment, specifically one of around 19Hz.[45]

< 53 >

The source of the infrasound in the workshop was traced to a fan in a laboratory cupboard. The sandstone cellar is in Coventry, England, and was originally beneath a fourteenth-century house owned by the Benedictine Priory that stood opposite, but is now below the Tourist Information Centre and is open to visitors. The staff at the centre became aware that a number of visitors were having disturbing experiences in the cellar. A Canadian journalist became frozen to the spot and was observed to turn "ashen" – he said that he felt as if a balloon was being pushed between his shoulder blades and had an intense feeling of a presence. He then reported seeing the face of a woman peering over his right shoulder. A Latvian tourist described feeling a presence and a cold chill. An American woman had such a strong sense of a presence that she refused to proceed further, feeling that some invisible thing was barring her way. The colour visibly drained from her face. A German-speaking tour guide felt a presence, as if she was disturbing something. She also felt a chill. There were many more examples. The effects were markedly similar in a wide range of people who otherwise knew nothing about a "ghost" nor of other people's reactions, and the sense of presence was felt by all witnesses in the same area of the cellar. Most people who visited, though, were not affected, so it seems as if only those with a certain sensitivity experienced the "ghost". (Indeed, according to an acoustic expert at Penn State University in the United States, it seems that some people are hypersensitive to infrasound.[46]) In England, Vic Tandy conducted repeated acoustic surveys and found a continuous dominant background 19Hz standing wave.[47] The signal was being modulated by a 2–4Hz signal. The source of the infrasound was not determined. If this kind of work can be extended and confirmed further, then there will be a strong basis for associating infrasound in certain environments with eerie, otherworldly sensations in suitably sensitive (or sensitized) people. There is clearly important research still to be done.

< 54 >

CHAPTER FIVE

Music to the Ears

Beyond ritual sounds, noises and simple percussive rhythms, there are the effects of what we would more readily recognize as music and song. Most people enjoy music, whatever their favourite kind happens to be, because it moves them emotionally, evokes spiritual feelings, inspires and consoles. But why? It is "just" patterned sound, after all. It is an enigma that has fascinated people for centuries. Even a brief dip into some of the ideas, observations and research music has generated provides insights into the deep roots that may underlie that more basic association between sound and ritual.

POETRY AND SONG

The poets of antiquity sang their verse rather than intoning it from a printed page. Psychologist Julian Jaynes states that accents on letters in poetry were sounded not by intensity stress as in our ordinary speech, but by pitch. In ancient Greece this pitch is thought to have been the interval of a fifth above the ground note of the poem, so that on the notes of our scale, dactyls (one long syllable followed by two short ones) would go GCC, GCC, with no extra emphasis on the G. Moreover, the three extra accents – acute(´), circumflex (ˆ) and grave (`) – were a rising pitch within the syllable, a rising and falling on the same syllable and a falling pitch, respectively. "The result was a poetry sung like plainsong with various auditory ornamentation that gave it a beautiful variety," Jaynes explained.[48]

Poetry was song – the human voice in league with music. The Celtic ideal was the bard and his harp – it is said that St Dunstan, the famed tenth-century abbot of Glastonbury in the West of England who converted to Celtic Christianity from paganism, carried a harp strapped to his back like some old druid, and that when he sang it was as if he were "talking with the Lord face to face". (It may be recalled that Weston La Barre maintained that music began with the singing of shamans.) One researcher, Mark Booth, has argued that song evokes primordial memories of the rhythms and vibrations of the womb – that it offers us moments of "authentic togetherness".[49] He goes on to propose the intriguing idea that song is so powerful in creating this sense because the marriage of music and words in song forces the two hemispheres of the brain to work in a specially unified way – speech being processed mainly by the left hemisphere, while the right primarily concerns itself with the processing of non-verbal sensibilities and communication, such as music. Some modification of this idea might not be a completely baseless notion: both brain hemispheres understand language, but in the Wada Test, in which a subject's left hemisphere is anaesthetized, the person cannot speak, *but can still sing*.

SYNAESTHESIA

Music, La Barre tells us, is "the perfect Rorschach stimulus for … meaning in reverie: we hallucinate meanings that are evoked only in the mind".[50] At some level or other, we know this to be true. Music can evoke images of mountains or caverns, oceans or wooded glades, and wild storms; it can conjure memories – a lover's face long ago in the candlelight of a restaurant, a moonlit walk by a beach, a moment of triumph or disaster. In some cases, it seems able to precipitate deep mystical states. It has truly been said that "music stands between spirit and matter".

While images flashing through the mind as a result of the sound of music is a relatively common and benign experience, the imagery can sometimes become truly hallucinatory. Perhaps the most dramatic effect of this kind is the phenomenon of synaesthesia, a phenomenon in which a susceptible person experiences one sensory stimulus in terms of another, so colours or coloured forms may be seen when

< 56 >

hearing a piece of music, or seeing a colour may give rise to the sensation of a particular smell, and so forth. The effect can also happen the other way round, so that the perception of a colour produces a sound or other intersensory effect. And visual perception may not even be involved – J.-K. Huysmans, for example, was apparently able to perform "voiceless melodies and mute funeral marches solemn and stately" to himself by mixing various liqueurs on his tongue![51] There are even cases of people who on experiencing one sensory stimulus will experience it in more than one other mode, so a sound might produce colours or shapes plus a scent or taste.

However, it is sound-to-vision that is the most reported form of synaesthesia, and it is sometimes referred to as "coloured hearing". It takes various forms: some people see soft tints of colour; others see colours appearing behind actual objects in the environment but without obscuring them; some see shapes and coloured shapes either with closed eyes or intense enough to blot out perception of the surroundings with open eyes. Some people live with synaesthesia on a permanent basis, while it happens sporadically with others. One writer described seeing on two occasions "radiant flashes of blinding colours and lights" during musical performances that he was wholly unprepared for and which did not repeat themselves at any other times.[52] There have been reports of the appearance of elaborate architectural forms being triggered by music, and even full-blown hallucinatory scenes.[53] Specific features of music, such as its loudness, rhythm and tempo, can affect how some synaesthetics experience their intersensory perceptions. The synaesthetic Russian composer Alexander Skriabin described how subdued music would produce merely "feelings" of colour in him, but louder music would be perceived as actual images.

While music is most usually the auditory trigger for this bizarre condition, non-melodic sounds, such as the beating of a gong, the ticking of a clock, the blowing of a whistle, and other such stimuli, have

< 57 >

been reported as producing synaesthesia, and in some subjects the human voice can provoke it as well. In speech, particular voices and intonation, or even specific vowels and consonants, have been claimed to provoke intersensory perceptions.

True, clinical synaesthesia is not some metaphorical or symbolic habit but genuine intersensory perception – a neurological phenomenon. Although it is usually considered a rare clinical condition, various surveys have, in fact, indicated that as much as 12 percent of any Western population is subject to it.[54] (Its occurrence in more traditional, non-Western societies seems not to have been adequately investigated.) Synaesthesia may exist on an even wider scale, albeit at a low, subliminal level, according to some studies. For example, in a 1940 experiment, a series of tones were played on a piano to more than 500 schoolchildren, and they were asked to select from a given range of colours for a "match" to each note. There was a remarkable unanimity among the children in their selections – "definitely greater than chance" – the experimenter, Louise Omwake, declared.[55]

Synaesthesia can be induced in virtually anyone who takes mind-altering drugs – indeed, it is a strong characteristic of the hallucinogenic experience, and is reported repeatedly in the relevant literature. In experiments with cannabis in 1924, Louis Lewin perceived distant sounds as "spherical". A few years later, Mayer-Gross and Stein, who were investigating the effects of mescaline, the active chemical in the psychoactive cactus peyote, reported that one of their subjects saw the sound of a metronome in colours. In another subject, the note C conjured up a red, F an orange-yellow, and higher tones brought about tints. The sound of chimes produced purple, and when the window-frame was repeatedly struck by an iron bar, the green of the foliage on trees outside turned lighter to the subject's perception on each impact.[56] There are countless other such drug-induced descriptions.

This fact raises some interesting matters with regard to the use of sounds in ritual, for ritualists are likely to be in trance states – often

< 58 >

produced by the ingestion of mind-altering plants (see Chapter 3). Synaesthetic perceptions could, therefore, be produced in response to drumming and singing during ritual activity. (In Chapter 9 it will be seen that musical stalactites in Palaeolithic caves have dots and daubs of colour painted on them, and it is feasible this is a result of such intersensory experience by the Stone Age cave ritualists.)

MUSICAL COMPOSITION IN TRANCE

While all this is speculative, studies of American Indians have shown with certitude that the composition of song and music can occur in trance. This happened particularly in the vision quest, a rite of passage for young men in which the individual went alone to some remote sacred place in the wilderness to fast and go without sleep for days at a time in order to receive a vision during the trance state that was produced. (In some tribes, this was a regular procedure by shamans, who often used mind-altering plants to aid the process.) It was – and is – during such quests that music was taught by spirit-beings to the visionary. "The spirit comes from afar and hits the ears; then it comes down the ears and stands in front of the person," explained one Flathead Indian. "It tells him what to do, and it sings the song." [57] Another Indian was left temporarily alone in the wild when only eight years of age. He described going "out of my head" and in the vision found himself on top of a mountain where people and animals were singing. He joined in with the songs and later became an important shaman. Wovoka, the Paiute prophet who instigated the Ghost Dance movement among American Indians at the end of the nineteenth century, also received songs in trance and taught them to his followers. On one occasion, after taking the Native American ritual sacrament of peyote, the hallucinogenic cactus, Wovoka _heard_ as well as saw the sun rise, and this auditory hallucination became a famous Indian song. Ethnomusicologist Alan Merriam deduces from such accounts that "hallucination and composition are closely connected". [58]

< 59 >

MUSIC AND EPILEPSY

In Chapter 3 it was noted that the anthropologist Donald Tuzin proposed that ritual instruments producing infrasound caused religious and visionary experiences by stimulating the temporal lobes of the brain; it is therefore perhaps not without significance that temporal lobe epilepsy can be triggered by music, and that there is a specific condition called "musicogenic epilepsy". This condition can also be accompanied by auditory hallucinations, an effect that may distantly relate to the phenomenon of musical composition in trance states. In a study of the hallucinatory effects afflicting temporal lobe epileptics, it was found that some 16 percent had auditory hallucinations prior to an epileptic seizure. Some people heard a beating sound – this was not a vague effect but "a commanding sensation as might be created by the whole of a brass section of the orchestra playing *fortissimo*".[59] Other hallucinatory sounds include bell-ringing, banging, ticking, and also rhythmical, melodic and verbal elements. It is thought that the composer Schumann, and possibly even Beethoven, suffered from auditory hallucinations.[60] Schumann was especially haunted, it is said, by the note A.

Musicogenic epilepsy was first described clinically in 1937, and is a form of epilepsy in which a seizure follows immediately after the patient is exposed to a particular stimulus – usually a complex piece of instrumental music in which many instruments are involved, such as a dance band or a full orchestra. In some cases it has been found that specifically the players of organs or pianos can suffer this form of epilepsy. Sometimes, the triggering stimulation can be very specific – one woman, for example, had seizures only when she heard Bach organ music, another only when she listened to one particular piece of music. Particularly emotionally moving music, where the person could be moved to tears, was also a trigger for some musicogenic epileptics. There is also a reflex epilepsy closely related to the musicogenic kind called audiogenic or sonogenic epilepsy in which non-musical sounds

< 60 >

such as the ringing of a telephone, the hissing of a kettle, or the whirring of machinery can provoke an attack.

Electroencephalogram (EEG) studies have shown that people with musicogenic epilepsy can show abnormalities in both left and right brain hemispheres, while in those with temporal lobe epilepsy an EEG disturbance is shown most often over the left hemisphere.[61] It was found that when seizures occured in musicogenic epileptics there tended to be an electrical brain discharge consisting of "bilateral synchronous elements" at 6Hz, steadily falling in frequency into the delta range (4Hz and lower) as the attack proceeded.[62] These are, of course, the very range of frequencies so often found associated with ritual rhythms, and it is perhaps no coincidence that shamanism and epilepsy have been related.[63]

PHYSICAL EFFECTS OF MUSIC

That music can affect physical processes in the body has been known since the early twentieth century, when scientific instrumentation began to be developed capable of adequately monitoring such changes.[64] The early work showed that, among other effects, listening to music can speed up bodily metabolism, produce exaggerated knee-jerks (in reaction tests), and have a marked effect on blood pressure and also the peripheral and central circulations. It was also shown that blood flow to the brain was increased under the influence of music.[65] In more recent times, detailed studies at Salzburg University have been able to put some finer detail on autonomic bodily reactions to music.[66]

CARDIOVASCULAR SYSTEM

Pulse rate was found to nearly always increase when the subject was listening to music – even when the same piece was repeated. Syncopated rhythms seem particularly capable of producing a higher pulse rate. There was also evidence that some musical sounds, such as drumming, could "drive" the pulse rate. Earlier claims to changes in blood pressure were confirmed.

< 61 >

RESPIRATION

Monitoring of subjects listening to passages of music show that not only do changes in the frequency and depth of breathing occur, but the relationship between inhalation and exhalation could change.

PSYCHOGALVANIC REFLEX (PGR)

PGR (the decrease of the electrical resistance of the skin) has proven to be a sensitive form of monitoring, and the modern work has confirmed earlier claims of such musically induced changes.

MOTOR ACTIVITY

By monitoring an increase in the number and amplitude of muscle-action potentials it was shown that muscular activity increases when a subject is listening to music. In one experiment, subjects were monitored for differences in integrated muscular activity between the forehead and the legs while being presented with a range of stimuli. They were asked to sequentially perform an arithmetical task, listen to Bach's *Brandenburg Concerto No. 6*, and then listen to dance music. Muscular activity was eighteen times more pronounced in leg muscles and up to five times more in the forehead region while listening to the Bach concerto than during the arithmetical task, and six times greater in the forehead and, surprisingly, over three times greater in the leg muscles than when listening to the dance music.

It was found that when a subject was asked to squeeze an ergometer (an instrument designed to measure the strength of the handgrasp) he was unable to carry out the task properly while music was being played. Lullabies invariably decreased muscular strength, while marching songs, predictably, increased it.

In an intriguing experiment, investigators found that autonomic responses in musical performers was even more marked than in listeners. They telemetrically monitored the pulse rate of the famous Austrian conductor Herbert von Karajan as he was conducting the

< 62 >

Leonora Overture No. 3. Care was taken to mask out any effects of physical exertion, and it was found that his pulse rate reached its highest frequencies (sometimes double the rate recorded at the beginning) during the passages in the music Karajan later identified as being those that had the greatest emotional impact on him. They did not correlate with moments of greatest physical effort in the conducting. When Karajan listened to a recording of the same piece of music, his pulse rate reacted in a similar way to when he was conducting, but the changes were not as great. The investigators later monitored Karajan's pulse rate as he carried out requested manoeuvres while piloting his own jet aircraft, but the responses were decidedly smaller than the music-induced effects.[67] Music really can manipulate our bodies.

MUSIC AND MYSTICISM

We must not think that it is only our modern engineers and scientists who have discovered that music can affect our physical and mental being – that understanding has been well known to certain types of mystics and holy people down the ages. Hazrat Inayat Khan, who died in 1927, was a Sufi teacher and musician, who came from an old musical family in Baroda, northwest India. One of his lectures was entitled "The Manifestation of Sound on the Physical Sphere". "The physical effect of sound has also a great influence upon the human body," he said. "The whole mechanism, the muscles, the blood circulation, the nerves, are all moved by the power of vibration. As there is a resonance for every sound, so the human body is a living resonator for sound ... Sound has an effect on each atom of the body ..."[68]

Inayat Khan went on to point out that drumming can cause ecstasy in people "because the sound of the drum goes directly into their whole system, bringing it to a certain pitch". Not technical language, perhaps, but an accurate account of what happens; he says it quite clearly – it is *pitch* that does the job, and pitch is frequency. He referred to a feast in

< 63 >

the Indian calendar when people are driven by drumming into an altered state called *hal* in which they are able to step into fires without being burned, or to cut themselves with blades and heal instantly. He likened this to the activities of the Rafai school of Sufis whose aim is to make the spirit gain mastery over matter. They, too, learn to subject themselves to flames and blades and yet remain unhurt. "The secret of the whole phenomenon is that by the power of words they try to tune their body to that pitch of vibration where no fire, no cut, nothing, can touch it."[69] It would seem from this that there are effects of sound upon the body that modern science has yet to discover. It is an area of research where it might prove profitable if science and spirituality came together.

< 64 >

1. *The Colossi of Memnon, Valley of the Kings, Egypt. One of the acoustic oracle sites frequented by ancient Greeks. The far statue in this view made strange sounds, probably due to cracks caused by an earthquake (Chapter 1).*

2. *Ancient American Indian rock carving at McCoy Spring, California, showing a shaman emerging from a crack in the rock as a snake and turning back into a man. This was how entranced shamans could contact the spirit world beyond the rock face. Spirits came from there as echoes (Chapter 1).* (David Whitley)

3. The Amazonian shaman, Ramón, with his ritual equipment. The bowl is for the mind-altering drink ayahuasca, and in his right hand is a schacapa leaf rattle. It was the sound of this rattle along with Ramón's whistling, whirring incantation that guided writer Tahir Shah on a remarkable visionary flight (Chapter 3). (Tahir Shah)

4. *The Treasury of Atreus tholos tomb, Mycenae, Greece (Chapter 6).*

5. *Inside the Treasury of Atreus. The door is 5.4 metres (more than 17 feet) tall. An acoustic effect like a buzzing of bees can be heard here – acoustic symbolism?*

6. *The amphitheatre at Epidaurus, Greece. A site with remarkable acoustics (Chapter 6).*

7. *The reconstructed Anasazi kiva at Aztec, New Mexico. This place inspired an acoustic investigation of megalithic sites in England and Ireland (Chapter 7).*

8. *The megalithic façade of Wayland's Smithy Neolithic tomb (Chapter 7).*

9. *Robert Jahn inside the cramped interior of one of Wayland's Smithy's chambers. The white object is an omnidirectional loudspeaker that produces a controlled spectrum of sound frequencies (Chapter 7).*

10. *The author recording acoustic readings outside the Chun Quoit Neolithic dolmen, Cornwall (Chapter 7).*

11. *Robert Jahn using a sound level meter in order to map standing waves inside the Chun Quoit chamber (Chapter 7).*

12. Inside the chamber of Cairn L, Loughcrew, Ireland, with its free-standing monolith (Chapter 7). Like other passage graves, the primary resonance of this chamber was within the frequencies of the adult male voice.

13. The passageway closing stone at Newgrange, Ireland, now fixed to the wall beside the entrance (Chapter 7). This could have affected sound in the entrance passage, or turned the tomb into an oracle site, or both.

14. The frontage of the Neolithic passage grave of Newgrange, Ireland. The entrance passage opens behind the carved stone. Note the "roof-box" opening above the passage's entrance lintel (Chapter 7).

15. *One of the giant, chiselled granite basins inside Newgrange (Chapter 7).*

16. *A range of rock-art inside the chamber at Newgrange – concentric rings, lozenge patterns, zigzags. Visible sound? (Chapter 7).*

CHAPTER SIX

Echoes of Ancient Knowledge?

What evidence do we have that ancient peoples considered acoustics when they built their sacred monuments? If in the ancient world sound was thought of as being so powerful, magical and sacred, then it would surely have been a considered factor in the establishment of a temple or sacred monument. The trouble with finding an answer to such a question is that we no longer have the "soundtrack" to the ancient past. When we visit the ancient places we wander around the ruins or the great stone structures trying to imagine the people who built these sites and worshipped at them, but we seldom hear them in our mind's ear. To attempt a remedy of that "time deafness", all we can do is grasp at what clues there are, either in the structures of the monuments themselves, or in whatever fragmentary documentary records have survived. Here are a few examples.

THE FROZEN MUSIC OF ANCIENT EGYPT

We know that sound could be used in magical ways in Egypt, and from hieroglyphs in tombs and temples scholars have been able to discover what instruments were used, but precious little is known about the architectural use of acoustics. It is a subject that has tended to slip through the fingers of mainstream research, to be found only in more esoteric quarters. There are claims that the ancient Egyptians used sonic means to levitate the stone blocks used to build the pyramids, and there have been observations that the geometrical precision which informs the structure of many Egyptian temples could conform to von Schelling's idea of architecture as "frozen music". While the first idea may be based on ignorance, this last notion may contain a germ of truth if a finding by writer John Anthony West is anything to go by. He has noted that a fallen obelisk in the great temple of Karnak, near present-day Luxor, can be made to produce sound. The obelisk, which broke when it fell, was fashioned from a single block of granite, but what had been its upper part, brought to a point by its pyramidion top, still forms a large piece. If the ear is placed to the angle of the pyramidion and the body of the obelisk is struck with the hand, "the enormous block resonates like a tuning fork at the slightest blow".[70] There is no way that this sonic property of cut granite would have been unnoticed by the Egyptian temple-builders – the only question is, did they cut obelisks and other architectural features to deliberate dimensions in order to produce the required sounds? Was there an acoustic element to their temple symbolism? West thinks it is likely, pointing out how carefully the Egyptians selected their building materials and the precision of their work.

"The obelisks were characteristically placed at the entrance to a temple and in a genuinely scientific manner attuned to the 'pitch' of that particular sacred site. It is impossible to say if this manifested itself on any detectable physical plane." [71]

Impossible, indeed, for there is, alas, no one to ask if any of this is true – there can now be only speculation.

GRECIAN AIRS

A similar tantalizing clue exists at a monument in Mycenae, Greece. It is a tholos tomb, known (mistakenly) as the Treasury of Atreus, dating to *c.*1250BC (see Plates 4 and 5). Tholos or "beehive" tombs were essentially stone-lined holes: a deep circular cut in a hillside was lined with blocks to create a beehive-shaped chamber with a corbelled dome ceiling. The doorway to it was approached by an entrance path or ramp cut through the hill slope and lined with stone walls. The dead were either laid out on or buried in the floor of the chamber. In the Treasury of Atreus the

< 66 >

doorway is 5.4 metres (more than 17 feet) high, and has a lintel weighing some 120 tons. The main chamber is 14.6 metres (nearly 48 feet) across and 13.5 metres (44 feet) high. It is an awesome structure.

No one knows the origin of the design of the tholos tomb, but the distinctive beehive shape might well be symbolic, for in ancient Greece the bee was associated with goddesses such as Demeter, and with immortality – it was thought the spirits of the dead could enter bees. Bees were also known as the "birds of the Muses", doubtless because of their buzzing. Is it a coincidence, then, that when just a solitary visitor quietly enters the chamber at the Treasury of Atreus and places an ear close to the great curving wall a buzzing sound can be heard – a buzzing like that of a swarm of bees, though a little softer? Was this supposed to be the spirits of the nobility being laid to rest there? The buzzing is an acoustic distortion of the distant background sounds of the outside world coming in through the doorway, probably akin to the effect of so-called "whispering galleries". There is an acoustic "dead spot" in the centre of the chamber.

We are often able to discern visual symbolism in the proportions, shapes and groundplans of ancient sacred buildings, but we are very slow in recognizing the likelihood that the ancient builders might also have employed acoustic symbolism. It is an issue that arises again more pointedly when we examine ancient Mayan acoustics (see Chapter 10).

The theories are on firmer ground with the later ancient Greeks, because it is known that they were acoustically aware. A classic site in this regard is the theatre at the healing complex, or Asklepion, of Epidaurus (see Plate 6). The theatre was built in the early third century BC and was designed by Polyklitos, perhaps a descendant of the great sculptor of the same name.

Set into a hillside, the vast auditorium is 130 metres (425 feet) across, and its fifty-five rows of seats could accommodate fully 12,000 people (though this was due to an expansion in the second century BC). The orchestra, which the semi-circular tiers of seating focus on, is nearly

< 67 >

20 metres (65 feet) in diameter. In its centre there is now just the base of a former altar to Dionysos. When a coin is dropped from knee-height onto this base it can be clearly heard from the top row of seats 59 metres (193 feet) away. It has been found that direct sound from the orchestra was augmented by reflection from the orchestra's floor and to a lesser degree from the vertical surfaces of the stage-house behind. Measurements in still air of word-articulation at Epidaurus yielded a value of 72 percent at the centre of the back row.

In addition to plays, great musical contests were held in the theatre. In the second century AD, Pausanias credited Polyklitos with the acoustic perfection of the theatre, indicating that those properties were recognized and valued.

ANCIENT ARCHITECTURAL ACOUSTICS

This appreciation of acoustics in late antiquity was a fact, as we can tell from the works of Vitruvius, the first-century BC Roman architect. For example, he drew on the use the Greeks supposedly made of "sounding vessels" (*echea*). These were bronze or clay vessels that were strategically placed within auditoriums to either amplify or deaden sound. Vitruvius wrote:

"...let bronze vessels be made on mathematical principles in keeping with the size of the theater, and have these vessels so made that when they are touched, they can produce among themselves the diatesseron [fourth], diapente [fifth], and so on, up to disdiapason [double octave]. Afterward place them in chambers set up for the purpose between the seats of the theatre. *"*[72]

He went on to instruct that the vessels, which should be tuned differently for different size theatres, should be placed upside down with a wedge under their orchestra-side rim tilting them back without touching any side of their special chambers, which should have an opening in them also facing the orchestra and which were to be located at specific points in the auditorium (see Figure 3). "By this contrivance ...

< 68 >

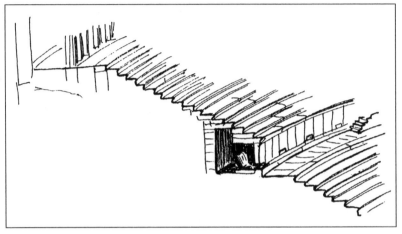

Fig. 3. *Sketch of a sounding vessel in place at the theatre of Aizanoi, Turkey*
(J. Durm, Baukunst der Griechen, *1910; reprinted from I. Rowland & T. Noble*
Howe, 1999, courtesy of Cambridge University Press)

the voice onstage … circling outward, strikes the hollows of the individual vessels on contact, stirring up an increased clarity and a harmonic complement of its own tone," the Roman architect wrote. Evidence for the use of sounding vessels has been found in up to sixteen archaeological sites.

Vitruvius also conceptualized the behaviour of sound in a way that is not too dissimilar to our modern understanding of waves: he saw it as radiating out from a source by the "endless formation of circles, just as endlessly expanding circles of waves are made in standing water if a stone is thrown into it". He considered echoes as being caused by obstructions to the circular, wavelike expansion of sound from a source. He additionally noted topographical factors to be taken into account in the siting of theatres that would aid the building's acoustics.

Around the same era in Scandinavia, and later, so-called boat-shaped timber longhouses were constructed. It has been assumed that these

< 69 >

were designed to mimic the shape of boats, though there have been doubts expressed about the adequacy of this explanation. The elongated structures had a marked outward bowing of their longer walls, and it is assumed that the roof-ridge had a corresponding arch. Good examples of the type are found in the groundplan post-hole traces at Trelleborg and Fyrkat in Denmark. One suggestion that has been offered by some scholars to explain their curious structural characteristics is that they would have provided good acoustics.[73] The truncated parabolic structural form would have provided acoustical foci at each end of the building, thus enhancing the distribution of sound throughout the hall. This may have been especially important, because it is known that the form of lyre used, a key musical instrument of the era, did not produce a sound sufficiently powerful to be heard well in large spaces. Were the boat-shaped buildings designed to amplify the output of such instruments, in addition to voices and other sounds? Experiments are under way to test the theory.

These "boat-shaped" houses may have developed from boat-shaped settings of standing stones that were built in Scandinavia from the late Bronze Age through to the Viking period. While boat symbolism is assumed, some of these sites – like the well-known Ales Stones overlooking the Baltic Sea in southern Sweden – also give distinctive local acoustical effects.

From medieval times, Gothic cathedrals stand out as superb examples of "frozen music"; studies of Chartres cathedral in France demonstrate that "they were undoubtedly envisaged at least in part as acoustic instruments".[74] Even more modest ecclesiastical buildings, such as St Gregory's Priory in Canterbury, England, have elaborate under-floor chambers that have not been shown to have anything to do with heating, drainage, or ventilation, and are suspected by some scholars to have been used to dampen low-frequency vibration.

The ritual sounds and music performed in such structures developed in symbiosis with the architecture. Did something similar happen

< 70 >

much earlier in the human story? Did the reverence, knowledge and use of sound go back to the megalithic monuments of the Stone Age – back, even, to the caves? Did people back then treat sound with awe, as a spiritual force? Was sound viewed as a powerful tool with which to produce trance and visions? Did sound become a factor in the way Stone Age people selected or built their sacred places? All is now silent, but in recent years some archaeological investigators have tried to find ways of using sound to probe into the mysteries of Stone Age sacred places, and some of these acoustical investigations are charted in Part Two. All the time, we need to keep in mind the rich history of humanity's complex relationship with sound and its effects.

< 71 >

PART TWO

Making the Old Stones Speak

The ruined sites of antiquity seem so eternal while sound is so much of the moment that acoustical investigation seems an unlikely archaeological tool. Yet any method of extracting knowledge about a site is of value, for there is no way of gaining information from prehistoric sites other than that which can be deduced directly from them by one technique or another. Acoustical probing offers another means of adding to the sum total of what is known about a place, and can perhaps enhance our insight into how ancient monuments may have been used. This section charts the acoustic enquiries taking place and outlines some of the theories that have been put forward. At last, archaeology is beginning to listen to the past.

CHAPTER SEVEN

Eavesdropping on the Stone Age

Purely by coincidence, two separate investigations into the acoustic properties of selected British and Irish Neolithic megalithic monuments commenced in the 1990s. Each research team was unknown to the other until the results were published. One was inspired, curiously, by a ceremonial site in the American Southwest, and the other by a Scottish stone circle.

RITUALS IN THE DARK

The first investigation began because of a visit to a thousand-year-old Anasazi *kiva* in New Mexico by Professor Robert Jahn, an applied physicist and aerospace engineer at Princeton University, along with the present author. At the time we were both taking part in field research for a programme under the aegis of the International Consciousness Research Laboratories (ICRL), an inter-disciplinary think-tank and research group.

The *kiva* was at the former Anasazi community of Aztec, near Farmington in northwest New Mexico. It had been restored to something like its original state (see Plate 7). To simulate what the atmosphere might have been like in Anasazi times, Hopi Indian songs and chants were piped into the reconstituted structure. Jahn drew attention to the notable acoustic qualities of the *kiva*. Could the shape and dimensions of *kiva*s have been determined by

Anasazi Kivas

The Anasazi formed a powerful American Indian culture whose members dominated the San Juan Basin, which extends across what is now known as the "Four Corners region", where the modern states of Utah, Colorado, New Mexico and Arizona meet. Their culture emerged in the final centuries BC but flowered from AD900 to 1300. The Anasazi Indians lived in flat-roofed, rectangular buildings made of adobe (sun-baked mud) and timber, which they developed into multi-storey terraces around plazas – an arrangement that still exists among today's communities of Pueblo Indians (the name deriving from *pueblo*, or "village" in Spanish, the language of the first Europeans to arrive here). The Anasazi people were great traders and builders, and they constructed mysterious roads for unknown purposes. They were also the originators of the *kiva*, a ritual or ceremonial chamber, usually large and circular, set into the ground and roofed over. Kivas were darkened places where the mysteries of the tribe were divulged. Activities in them would have included chanting, smoking, storytelling and theatrical ceremonial displays. There would also have been secret ritual activity, probably involving the use of mind-altering plant substances like *Datura* (jimson weed), as is known to have occurred in the smaller *kiva*s of the Pueblo peoples who may be the descendants of the Anasazi.

empirical observations made by the Anasazi as to how to make their chants and ceremonial songs sound as powerful and resonant as possible?

< 76 >

SIMPLIFIED CHRONOLOGY OF PREHISTORY

PALAEOLITHIC
(Old Stone Age)
 Lower   *c*.2.5 million–*c*.80,000BC
  (first signs of human
  activity, hand-axes)
 Middle   *c*.80,000–*c*.33,000BC
  (Neanderthals, stone-flake
  tools, cave dwellings)
 Upper   *c*.33,000–*c*.8500BC
  (*Homo sapiens*, rock-art,
  stone technology)

MESOLITHIC   *c*.8500–*c*.4000BC
(Middle Stone Age)

NEOLITHIC   *c*.4000–*c*.2000BC
(New Stone Age)

BRONZE AGE   c.2000–c.800BC

IRON AGE   *c*.800BC–historic era

It was a reasonable idea, and Jahn doodled with a stick in the sandy floor as he listened and ruminated, drawing wave-like patterns. More familiar with the prehistoric sites of the British Isles, I thought that it would be interesting to test that idea in the vaguely similar but much older and more enigmatic megalithic tombs of Neolithic Europe (see the box above for approximate dates). These would also be a more challenging proposition, because there was no surviving knowledge about the societies that had built them nor what they had really been

< 77 >

Megalithic Tombs

"MEGALITHIC" = GREEK: *MEGAS*, LARGE, *LITHOS*, STONE

These major, visible monuments are found widely within western Europe. They date to the Neolithic era, and include a number of main structural types: basic, stone, box-like features (dolmens) once covered or partially covered by mounds of earth or stones; elongated burial chambers reached by a short entrance area or vestibule (gallery graves, *allées couvertes*), found in France; long, chambered mounds with a curved frontage enclosing an open courtyard area (court cairns); and great mounds containing, usually, large chambers accessed by one or more passages (passage graves). The chambers in this latter type of monument are often of cruciform shape, with the passage entering a main chamber off which there are side-chambers. There are also a number of other megalithic tomb designs that are variations on these themes. These features belong to the overall Neolithic monument-building tradition, which produced standing stones, stone circles and earthworks, such as henges.

While bones were certainly deposited in most megalithic tombs, it is by no means certain that burial was the tombs' sole function – and perhaps not even the main one. Features such as passages indicate that there was a need for repeated access during a site's heyday, and forecourts suggest gatherings of some kind. So the monuments may have been more like temples than tombs and were perhaps used for rituals related to the spirits of the ancestors. Because of their architectural similarities, it is reasonable to assume that all passage graves are related, emerging from some common source, but materials found in them are seemingly always of relatively local origin. This suggests the possibility of there having been a widespread cult.

< 78 >

used for. Anything extra that could be found out about them would be a bonus. So a plan was hatched to conduct a preliminary field study in Britain and Ireland as soon as the resources could be found.

The ICRL field investigation got underway in 1994. Its aim was to check the acoustical resonances of a small but representative sample of megalithic chambered mounds, but with the emphasis on the "passage grave" type (see box, left).

Apart from deciding to include one of the largest and earliest passage graves of them all – Newgrange in Ireland – it was agreed to take what was effectively a random selection of chambered mounds, determined simply by the limited resources of time and finances available. The field study began at Wayland's Smithy, a chambered barrow on the Berkshire downs, in southern England. It owes its name to an old legend stating that a spectral blacksmith called Wayland inhabits the site and that travellers' horses left overnight near the monument will be found magically shod by morning. The barrow sits within a group of trees in a dramatic location just off the Ridgeway, a prehistoric trackway that is now a rural leisure route. Wayland's Smithy consists of an earthen mound 55 metres (176 feet) long that tapers at the rear end. The front has a megalithic façade made up of massive upright sarsen stones from between which a stone passageway some 6.7 metres (21 feet) long leads into the mound (see Plate 8). This, in fact, forms part of the burial chamber, and near its end there are two side-chambers that form a kind of megalithic transept and give the whole chamber a cruciform plan. The side-chambers are small, less than 2 metres (6 feet) in any direction. When excavated, the chamber was found to contain eight human skeletons, including one of a child. Prior to this long mound and megalithic chamber there had been a timber mortuary hut on the site which had contained fourteen bodies; some of these were whole skeletons and others had separated limbs, suggesting that they had originally been placed elsewhere, perhaps while they defleshed. This earlier feature is now covered by the existing mound.

< 79 >

The working procedure adopted at Wayland's Smithy, as at all the subsequent sites, was to set up a sound source (an omnidirectional loudspeaker). This was placed on the floor, or mounted on a short tripod, and driven by a variable frequency sine-wave oscillator and a 20-watt amplifier, with the sound frequency verified by an external, handheld, digital multimeter. The amplitude of soundwaves in the various chambers the ICRL team visited was mapped with a portable sound-level meter sensitive to between 55 and 105 decibels. The frequency coming from the sound source was manually swept through the lower audible range until the lowest natural resonance of the chamber became clearly discernible. When this was established, the loudness was adjusted to the highest comfortable level, and a measured grid or measuring tape was laid on the ground from the sound source out to the walls of the chamber. This enabled radial horizontal surveys of the acoustic standing waves within the chamber to be made with the sound-level meter.[75] If the frequency of the sound was set accurately at whatever the natural primary resonance of each chamber was, it was to be expected that there would be a series of antinodes (soundwave crests, or points of maximum amplitude) and nodes (troughs between wave crests, or points of zero amplitude), with a primary antinode at the wall of the chamber, because a standing wave within a chamber is created by the sound reflecting off the wall back towards the source, thus causing two soundwave patterns to be superimposed one on the other, making it appear to be a stationary wave pattern.

Working at Wayland's Smithy was difficult due to the smallness of the chamber complex, which made for cramped conditions (see Plate 9). However, a partial survey was completed. The east side-chamber resonated most strongly at 112Hz and the west chamber at 95Hz. A secondary resonance was identified in the east side-chamber at 119Hz. These results were noteworthy, as these frequencies sit squarely within the adult male vocal range. How strange to find such resonances here, in a place presumably intended for the silent dead! It was assumed that this was probably a coincidental set of results.

< 80 >

The next stop for the ICRL team was in the very different, much wilder, environment of Cornwall in the extreme southwest of England. The site targeted there was Chun Quoit, a now-exposed dolmen that stands on an isolated ridge (see Plates 10 and 11). Dated to *c.*3500BC, Chun Quoit consists of four inward-leaning slabs topped by a capstone that weighs several tons, and it appears never to have been entirely covered by a mound. The interior space was roughly a cube with sides measuring 1.5 metres (5 feet). No bones or artefacts were found inside the structure when it was excavated.

The composite resonance frequency of Chun Quoit was found to be 110Hz, right in the baritone range – the second lowest level of the male singing voice. The team had now found the same frequency range occurring at two sites. A coincidence?

While in Cornwall, the temptation could not be resisted to visit an example of one of the county's most enigmatic monument types, officially named souterrains but known locally as *fogous*. The ICRL team chose the Carn Euny *fogou*, which is located beneath the remains of an Iron Age village of that name. It consists of a stone-lined tunnel running down from the earth's surface to slightly underground. Uniquely, the Carn Euny *fogou* has a low, short passage to the side and leading into a circular chamber that once had a corbelled roof to form a beehive-shaped structure. Most *fogous* are just stone tunnels, and their function is a matter of some controversy. The official view is that they were storage places for root crops, though another theory is that they were refuges for villagers in times of danger. No conclusive evidence for or against these views has been found. A more contentious theory is that they were ritual chambers (somewhat akin to *kivas*, though of a cruder nature).[76] No one knows for sure. At Carn Euny, the beehive feature is dated to *c.*500BC, and the tunnel to a little later. If *fogous* are a mystery, then the beehive structure is even more of one. It could have served a ritual function more readily than the tunnel, yet nothing was found in it when it was excavated – there is simply an enigmatic niche

< 81 >

in the wall, unconnected to a flue or other feature and therefore not a fireplace, which it is hard not to think of as a recess for a votive object – a kind of altar.

Although this site was not a Neolithic megalithic tomb, the ICRL team's main research concern, an acoustic investigation was made of it. Intriguingly, the beehive structure was found to resonate at 99Hz – again comfortably within the male vocal range. This was interesting on two counts: one was that here once more was a resonance in the vocal range and, second, if these acoustic findings were to be interpreted as indicative of the function of the beehive chamber, then they would support the ritual contention. But enough time had been spent on this dalliance, and the main field research had to continue.

Logistic problems intervened to prevent an intended check of one or two more English passage grave sites, and with time running short the team had to make haste to Ireland. There, it headed first for the Loughcrew Hills in County Meath, about an hour's drive northwest of Dublin. Because there are numerous Neolithic chambered cairns (stone mounds) scattered along a hill ridge at this location, it was an obvious place to visit. Legend has it that a witch was flying over the hills carrying big boulders in her apron, but she dropped some and they became the cairns. Another story suggests that a place near the cairns was an oracle site.

The first site selected was the impressive Cairn L. It has an imposing entrance and a 5-metre (16-feet) passageway leading into a large central chamber, 6 metres (19 feet) across and 3 metres (10 feet) high, off which there are several side-chambers. A unique feature of this site is that the chamber contains a free-standing monolith (see Plate 12). There have been claims that this is illuminated by the November sunrise (one of the old Celtic cross-quarter days) – the near horizon and angle of the entrance passage apparently combine to admit just a narrow sunbeam that spotlights the pale-coloured standing stone in the darkened chamber.[77] One of the side-chambers contains a large but shallow stone basin and a

< 82 >

Fig. 4. Stone basin and rock art in Cairn L, Loughcrew (J. Fergusson, Rude Stone Monuments, *1871)*

considerable amount of intriguing rock-carvings (see Figure 4). The team would not hazard a guess what the resonance frequency of such a complex interior would turn out to be, and took eight radial surveys out from the central sound source. The team members did not know whether to be surprised or not when the primary resonance frequency turned out to be 110Hz. Each of the shallower side-chambers had an antinode at its outer wall with an associated node just inside its opening, and the one deeper side-chamber, opposite the entrance passage, displayed two antinodes and two nodes. Considering that yet another vocal-range frequency had been discovered, the team quietly felt that it was perhaps not too surprising that there were old legends of ancient oracle stones in the area.

Cairn I, nearby, was also checked acoustically. This site no longer has a roof, but the wall stones are still intact. There are carved patterns on some of them, and the passage aligns to the prominent Cairn T situated on a distant peak. The resonance frequency was 112Hz.

Forty-eight kilometres (30 miles) east from Loughcrew is the Boyne Valley, containing a rich crop of mighty megalithic monuments. Three of the most famous of these are the passage graves of Knowth, Newgrange and Dowth. The ICRL team's destination was Newgrange, for which special access permits had been obtained. The great mound of Newgrange stands some 11 metres (36 feet) high and 90 metres (300 feet) in diameter. Around its base is a kerbing of ninety-seven stones, which act as a retaining wall. Three of these stones are extensively decorated by carvings, and a few others have limited markings. Placed horizontally in front of the mound's entrance is a stone (kerbstone 1) incised with a rich variety of spiral and lozenge designs (see Plate 14). The entrance gives access to a passage 18.9 metres (62 feet) long, ending in a corbelled stone chamber 7 metres (20-feet) high. The passage averages about 1.5 metres (5 feet) in height and its floor rises steadily from the entrance to the chamber, which has three side-chambers or recesses, one at its rear (opposite to where the passage enters the chamber) and one at either side. Large stone basins were found in these recesses (see Plate 15). Many fragments of both burned and unburned human bones were found in various parts of the chamber complex, but these appeared to add up to the remains of only a few individuals. Newgrange has been dated to *c.*3200BC, making it considerably older than Egypt's Great Pyramid (dated to *c.*2585BC) and one of the oldest roofed structures in the world.

The monument's entrance aligns to the rising winter solstice sun, providing one of the most dramatic examples of ancient astronomical knowledge. There is a curious rectangular opening above the passage entrance. The top lintel of this structure, an

< 84 >

engraved slab, had been visible prior to excavations, but site archaeologist Michael J. O'Kelly revealed the full nature of what he called the "roof-box" (see the picture of the entrance in Plate 14). On 21 December each year a pencil beam of direct sunlight shoots through the roof-box and along the passage. It creeps across the chamber floor as far as the basin stone in the end recess. Because of precession (the Earth's slow axial "wobble"), the sun's rising position at midwinter has moved slightly and this means the sunbeam entering through the roof-box cannot now reach to the very back of the end recess as it would have done originally. As the sunbeam slowly rotates across the floor, like the illuminated hand of a clock, the whole chamber lights up with the golden glow of the reflected sunlight. Direct sunlight through the passage doorway cannot reach as far as the chamber because of the upward slope of the passage floor and the arrangement of the upright stones or "orthostats" forming the passage walls.

The monument was an impressive final site on the ICRL team's itinerary, and it demanded some time for the acoustic survey to be completed. As the team members progressed along each radial survey line out from the sound source, the ample space in the chamber made it easier than usual for them to actually hear the soundwave pattern, in the sense that at the nodes or troughs the sound tone being emitted by the loudspeaker became very faint, and would then increase as the next wave "rose" to its antinode or crest. (Someone unfamiliar with the details of the wave structure of sound propagation in an enclosed resonant space might readily, but mistakenly, assume that the sound would diminish at a regular rate in keeping with the distance out from the sound source – as it would in an open space.) This meant that although only a few metres from the sound source, locations could be found in the chamber that were effectively silent, which contrasted rather eerily with the loud, throbbing sound at antinode points. The chamber complex was found to resonate at what had by now become

< 85 >

the virtually expected 110Hz (see Figure 5). The classic passage grave site had the "classic" natural primary resonance frequency.

The passage presented a fascinating acoustical situation of its own. Soundwaves driven into the passage from the chamber were found to produce, due to partial reflection from the stones surrounding the entrance to the passage, a standing wave pattern along its whole length, displaying twelve antinode/node pairs and acting rather like a musical wind instrument (see Figure 6). The wave naturally lessens in amplitude the further from the sound source it travels (that is, the loudness of the sound decreases), ultimately passing out through the passage entrance to dissipate in open space beyond. There is, however, an intriguing feature at Newgrange that is rarely mentioned: a separate slab of rock that exactly fits the aperture of the passage entrance, theoretically capable of being put in place and removed as required (see Plate 13). If this closing stone was fixed in place on the – presumably – occasional times when ritualists entered the monument, then any sounds they made would have created a more intense standing wave within the passage. If this was the case, the deep, otherworldly sounds from the inner sanctum of the mound would have emerged with particular power out through the roof-box – perhaps at the time the winter solstice sunbeam was entering through it. This would have created an alchemical exchange of light and sound: regenerating solar light for the ritualists and the ancestral spirits within, awesome sounds announcing the cosmic moment for the congregation outside.

PRIMARY IMPLICATIONS

The ICRL field research was simply a pilot study, and subsequent work has not been undertaken at the time of writing, though new acoustic instrumentation has been purpose-designed and built in preparation for a fresh wave of research.[78] Nevertheless, the work done so far does present some tantalizing potential implications.

< 86 >

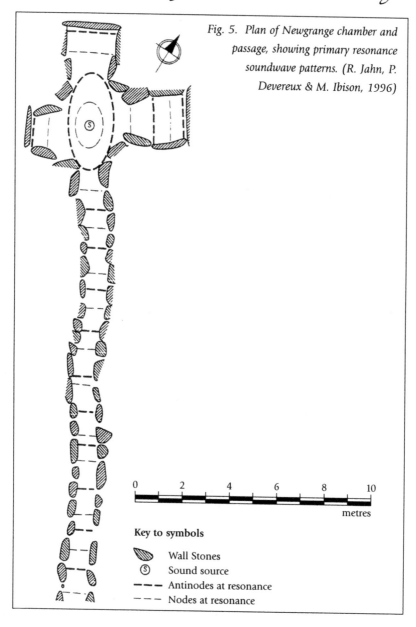

Fig. 5. Plan of Newgrange chamber and passage, showing primary resonance soundwave patterns. (R. Jahn, P. Devereux & M. Ibison, 1996)

Key to symbols

Wall Stones
(S) Sound source
– – – Antinodes at resonance
– – – Nodes at resonance

< 87 >

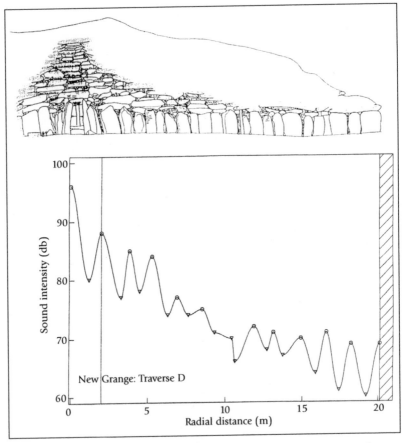

Fig. 6. Elevation of Newgrange passage (top) and primary resonance soundwave pattern along the passage (below)

Although many more chambered tombs need to be tested before a statistical evaluation can be properly attempted, it is at least suggestive that, despite the various monuments being of markedly different sizes, shapes and construction, all the sites visited in the study yielded resonance frequencies in a narrow band (95–120Hz), most often

< 88 >

clustering in the precise zone of 110–112Hz. If rituals involving singing or chanting did take place in these kinds of monuments, then it could be expected that as a result of empirical experience the chambers would very likely have been constructed to the optimum dimensions, because singing or uttering oracular pronouncements at the resonance frequency of a chamber would enhance the volume and reverberation of the voice. Such a maximized vocal effect would be appropriate for creating the commanding sense of the presence of supernatural agencies, whether gods or ancestral spirits. Moreover, the male voice in the frequency range concerned can generate a high intensity.

If these chambers were designed solely for the silent dead, it is odd that they should repeatedly be found to be so ideally suitable for the performance of the living human voice. The potential implication is quite clear: *these "tombs" saw ritual activities, and they were conducted by men.*

ROCKING ON

Dozens of theories have sought to explain the meaning of prehistoric rock-art. Professor Jahn came up with another. As he looked around the Newgrange chamber, he was fascinated by the profusion of carved patterns on the walls and ceilings – curious carved indentations, spirals, concentric circles, lozenge designs and zigzag lines make the surrounding rock-surfaces appear to seethe with activity (see Plate 16). It occurred to him that the circular motifs looked rather like the plans the ICRL team was producing of the resonant sound patterns within the chamber, and the zigzag motifs looked like the sinusoidal arrangement of the alternating nodes and antinodes found in the radial traverses out from the sound source. Two particular zigzag carvings on the left side of the western side-chamber particularly caught his eye because they had the same number of "nodes" and "antinodes" as the resonant standing-wave pattern the team had mapped from the chamber centre out along the passage. Could at least some of these enigmatic carvings have related to the acoustical environment in the monument at ritual

< 89 >

times? At first glance this seems an unlikely proposition, but on further analysis it looks less improbable.

The main issue is, how could the Stone Age ritualists at Newgrange have imaged the soundwaves? It was already demonstrable that in theory they could have heard the pattern, but while that may conceivably have given them the idea of concentric circles, it would not have given them the image of a zigzag (waveform) pattern. For that, they would have had to have been able to see the soundwaves. But how? Two possible ways come to mind: one is by means of trance-induced synaesthesia (see Part One), and the other is by means of the winter solstice sunbeam shining through a smoke or mist of some kind within the chamber and passage while chanting or singing at the primary resonance frequency was taking place. How would this have worked?

First, the "mist". A large number of rituals around the world are accompanied by incense smoke or, at the very least, the smoke from a fire, and this is one way the "mist" might have been created; but another possibility is the presence of steam. There is an old Irish tradition of the *fulachta fiadh*.[79] These features are "burnt mounds" which mark the remains of sites where water was once heated by hot stones. The dates of these sites span the period from the prehistoric Bronze Age into the historic era, and they are found by the hundreds in the British Isles – at Drombeg, for example, in association with a stone circle. Tests have shown that rocks heated in a fire can bring 454 litres (100 gallons) of cold water to boiling point within half an hour. Conservative opinion claims that the sites were used for cooking (meat can be cooked effectively by this means), but there is also evidence to indicate that they could have been for bathing – saunas, in fact.[80] When this interpretation is placed against archaeological findings that indicate structures similar to wigwams were sometimes erected at sites in Ireland (for example at Ballyvourney), the image of something akin to an American Indian sweatlodge comes to mind. It is possible that

< 90 >

such sites had combined functions – for instance, an eighteenth-century Irish manuscript, *The Romance of Mis and Dudh Ruis*, describes the use of a pit to heat water, first for cooking and then for washing and bathing.[81] American Indian sweatlodges were, of course, ritual sites, where altered mind states accompanied bodily purification. It has been suggested by various commentators that the large shallow bowls found in the chamber complex at Newgrange may have been intended for holding water. If water and hot stones were indeed placed in these at times of important rituals, such as at the winter solstice, then steam would have filled the chamber and passage, revealing with stark clarity the crucial midwinter sunbeam lancing in through the roof-box. A similar effect would have been created if the interior had been filled with incense smoke.

If chanting or singing was taking place, then the soundwaves – which are physical phenomena – would have vibrated the aerosol components, whether water molecules or minute smoke particles. Illuminated by the laser-like beam of the penetrating sun, dark, shifting shapes would have been produced due to the particles being organized by vibration into the pattern of the soundwaves. These could easily have been interpreted by the ritualists as the ancestral spirits floating in the air in response to their chanting. A group of priests, or, more likely, a shaman, might be visualized, perhaps wearing animal skins and an antler headdress, drumming and chanting while crouched in the deep darkness of the chamber, perhaps after having drunk infusions made from mind-altering plants, communing with the spirits of the revered ancestors whose bones lay grouped around, waiting for the entry of the beam of sunlight that would have signalled the turning of the dark point of the year and bringing hope of rebirth and renewal. As the sunbeam shone in, dark forms (the sound patterns) would have been seen floating and writhing in its golden ray – proof that the ancestral spirits were stirring within the sacred confines of the monument.

< 91 >

In order to demonstrate that it was possible such phenomena would have been visible, Jahn's Princeton Engineering Anomalies Research (PEAR) laboratory at the university made a working model of the Newgrange passage. Ironically, the passage is the megalithic equivalent of a Kunst tube – a standard laboratory device specifically designed to disclose in a visible fashion the action of soundwaves. The experimental model comprised a Plexiglass tube nearly 2 metres (6 feet) long, sealed at one end and with sound pumped through from the other end (see Plate 17). Inside, a special kind of dust doubled for the actual smoke or steam of the hypothesized ritual situation. Sure enough, when the experimental apparatus was switched on, the airborne dust particles clearly vibrated to reveal the acoustic standing-wave within the tube when an intense beam of light simulating the sunbeam was shone through them, presenting a scaled-down version of what actually could have happened in the Newgrange passage.

ORACLE CHAMBERS

Another vision of an acoustic ritual at Newgrange was put forward as early as 1969 by archaeologist Frances Lynch. She pointed out that the long period of usage Newgrange and other passage graves appear to have been subjected to suggests that something more than mere funerals must have taken place at them, especially in light of the fact that relatively few individuals seem to have been buried in them. She suggested that the closing stone at Newgrange had been a permanent seal to the passageway, inserted after the last funeral had taken place, noting that various other methods of blocking off were used in many other passage graves in Ireland and Britain. According to Lynch, it was the roof-box that became the focal point for subsequent ritual at Newgrange and not the chamber complex. O'Kelly had found that the roof-box had been blocked with two moveable quartz blocks, and scratch-marks on top of the passage entrance lintel show these blocks

< 92 >

had been moved out on many occasions. The roof-box had been repeatedly opened up – but why? It is too small to allow ready access by adults, so physical entry into the mound was probably not its function. It might have been for the placing of offerings, yet there were no archaeological traces of any such deposits, rendering this an unlikely explanation.[82] Lynch wrote:

> *"* I would like to suggest that this narrow slot in a complex, hollow stone structure could have been used as some form of oracle. People might seek the advice of their ancestors by asking their questions through the slot and their distorted words would come back to them as an answer, of which they could make what they liked. *"*[83]

Frances Lynch presented evidence to show that the passage in cruciform passage graves, and in certain other designs of passage grave as well, may have acted as a means of communication rather than of access. Sites she mentioned included Site L in the Boyne Valley complex, the majority of the chambered cairns of Loughcrew, Fournocks – also in County Meath – and Baltinglass in County Wicklow, all in Ireland; Barclodiad y Gawres and Bryn Celli Ddu on the island of Anglesey in Wales; West Kennet long barrow at Avebury in England; and Maes Howe in Orkney, Scotland.

Although the roof-box feature is unique to Newgrange, she found variable evidence that at other sites the passages had been constructed in two distinct ways – a simpler outer part, usually low and unroofed, which was filled in as a closing procedure, leaving a space exposed beneath the first lintel of a more structured inner passage. This provided a small opening for the sort of activities she suggested may have taken place at the Newgrange roof-box.

While the ICRL team feel that their model of acoustic phenomena at Newgrange is the most likely, it does not necessarily preclude a later manifestation of the kind Lynch describes, perhaps as the knowledge of the original activities of the site declined in the folk memory with the passage of generations. Lynch's theory could

< 93 >

Fig. 7. A dolmen with a "spirit hole" in India.
(J. Fergusson, Rude Stone Monuments, *1871)*

certainly apply to dolmens possessing so-called "spirit holes" in their entrance stones – a feature found at such sites as widely separated as Germany and India (see Figure 7).

CIRCLES OF SOUND

When one of the papers resulting from the ICRL team's preliminary acoustic investigations was published in 1996 in an archaeological journal,[84] it became known that two researchers from Reading University were also engaged on acoustic explorations of megalithic sites: Aaron Watson, then a postgraduate archaeology student, and David Keating, then a professor in the university's cybernetics department. The pair's work

< 94 >

had been inspired by a chance visit Watson had made in 1994 to the stone circle of Easter Aquorthies in Aberdeenshire, Scotland (see Plate 18), which is 19.5 metres (62 feet) in diameter. The site is one of the district's many "recumbent" stone circles, a term that refers to the presence of a large, altar-like horizontal stone set in a ring of otherwise upright standing stones. The function of these enigmatic sites is unknown. Watson first became aware of the possibilities of extracting acoustic information from megalithic monuments when he noticed that he could hear clearly what other people were saying as they moved around the circle. There was a "peculiar echo" being reflected across the circle from the recumbent stone and its flanking uprights situated on the southerly side of the circle. The large block seemed to be boosting the sound and projecting it across the interior of the ring of stones. This projection of sound was not uniform: it could be heard easily in some areas, but was faint in others. In addition, subtler reverberations appeared to originate from different places around the circle. Watson wondered what the site's builders would have made of these effects, and suspected that they had probably been viewed as magical or supernatural phenomena.

Later, after enlisting Keating's expert assistance, an acoustic study was made of the monument. The approach of the Reading University duo differed from that of the ICRL team. Watson and Keating deployed an amplifier and a digital audio tape recorder with an omnidirectional microphone fixed to a tripod. The amplifier was placed in the alcove formed by two stones that projected out from the face of the recumbent stone and was set to continuous "pink noise", which sounds rather like a distant waterfall. Pink noise was used because it has a wide range of frequencies likely to include those that would have been produced by people or musical instruments in the Stone Age. Recordings were made over a 2 metre (6 feet) grid laid out across the interior area of the circle. The recordings were converted into decibels using a real-time spectrum analyser. A control experiment using the same equipment and procedure but in an open space was also conducted.

< 95 >

The control experiment showed the expected uniform decay of sound in keeping with the distance from the sound source. By contrast, the pattern of sound energy within the Easter Aquorthies circle presented a much more complex picture. The set-up was reminiscent of a theatre, with the sound made within the recumbent alcove being clearly projected towards the interior of the circle like a sound coming from a stage or rostrum. The echo effect Watson had picked up on his initial visit showed up in the printed survey as a tight ripple of plotted acoustic contours. The subtle reverberations he had noticed did not show up on the survey, however, and the Reading team considered this might be because they were due to sound reflection between a person standing within the circle and the surrounding stones. The survey confirmed that the distribution of stronger sound was distinctly and almost precisely contained within the ring of stones. Anyone outside the perimeter of the monument would have remained largely unaware of the acoustic effects within – a charmed circle.

The meaning behind the recumbent circles has long attracted speculation. Most of it has been based on visual characteristics, such as the fact that many of the monuments have stones of graded heights, becoming taller towards the recumbent stone, and that the recumbent stones are so positioned as to orient towards the moon at key times in the lunar cycle. But judging by the Reading team's findings, there is clearly a need for further consideration of their acoustic properties too. The theatre-like arrangement, with the recumbent stone like a rostrum or stage, and the tallest stones being placed around it with others grading down in height from them towards the opposite side of the circle, presents obvious acoustic possibilities. Whatever the rites were that took place at Easter Aquorthies, the chief officiant must surely have stood before the recumbent stone, the better to maximize the power of his or her voice (or sound-making device). The acoustical findings conjure a virtual ghost of a priest or priestess standing there, leading rituals whose pressing importance has paled with the passing of the millennia.

< 96 >

HUMMING A TOMB

Having cut their acoustic research teeth on a stone circle, the Reading pair decided to investigate a passage grave. They chose the Camster Round in Caithness, Scotland (see Plate 19). It is 17.5 metres (55 feet) in diameter and has a central chamber of 3 metres (10 feet), accessed from the outside by a narrow passage some 6 metres (19 feet) long. The passage opens into an antechamber from where the chamber proper is entered. This circular cairn is a companion to a linear cairn nearby called Camster Long.

The procedure at Camster Round was initially the same as at Easter Aquorthies, with pink noise being generated and a tape-recorded survey made of the interior (see Plate 20). Three main effects were noted: because the sound reflected off the chamber walls it was amplified and echoes were created, sound was transmitted along the passage, and outside the tomb sound could be heard emerging from the passage entrance but it faded away markedly by the time it reached the edge of the entrance forecourt, which had been an original feature of the cairn. When the researchers walked around the outer perimeter of Camster Round they found that internal sound could be heard easily in some places but not in others. It was concluded that this had to be due to different densities of the material constituting the cairn, or else to interference patterns caused by soundwaves travelling around the edges of the tomb. When a range of frequencies was broadcast within the chamber, these disparities were rendered more obvious.

Next, the team broadcast a range of frequencies within the chamber using a tone generator much in the manner of the ICRL team – save that the Reading pair were trying out standing waves at various frequencies rather than simply establishing the natural primary resonance of the chamber. At certain pitches, the sound behaved in noteworthy ways: among these was how the source of the emitted tone could become unclear, appearing to issue from different parts of the chamber – sometimes the sound actually seemed to be inside listeners' heads. Another effect was that at certain frequencies even small physical

< 97 >

movements by listeners could create marked variations in volume and pitch. A special case of this was that anyone approaching through the passageway could be sensed by people inside the chamber because the mass of the person's body created microtonal disturbances in the sound distribution. Speech within the chamber was found to become seriously distorted, resulting in some "extraordinary harmonics".[85]

Importantly, it was demonstrated that a group of people vocalizing a continuous note could produce the same acoustic effects as the electronic sound generator. These effects could, therefore, have been produced by the Stone Age people who had built the monument.

THE BEAT GOES ON

The Reading team also experimented with drumming inside the chamber. The sound of the drumming passed most effectively down the passage, and could be heard outside in the forecourt. Away from the passage entrance, the sound became more distorted. The higher frequencies were filtered out by the cairn structure, leaving the bass notes enhanced – somewhat like the throbbing beat that can heard from outside a motor vehicle when the driver has rock music playing loudly on the stereo system inside it. At places around the circumference of the cairn the interior drumming sounded "deep and unfamiliar", and it sometimes seemed to rise up from the ground rather than from the tomb itself, an effect the investigators found "quite striking".[86]

The researchers then went on to make a truly remarkable discovery. Generally speaking, the sound made inside the chamber at Camster Round did not travel far beyond the site due to both the dampening effect of the cairn's structural material and background sounds such as the wind. On the day the tests were conducted, the maximum limit of audibility was about 100 metres (328 feet) from the cairn. Yet inside the chambers of neighbouring Camster Long, about twice that distance away, the drumming in Camster Round could be heard as a subtle, distant "booming" sound, which appeared to rise from the long cairn's floor. The

< 98 >

longer wavelengths of the low frequencies of the drumming had somehow managed to travel and be audible in the calm air inside Camster Long in a way that was not possible in the open air.

On the basis of this unexpected finding, Watson and Keating have speculated that this effect could have been exploited in places where chambered mounds occur in close proximity.[87] Many of the larger passage graves, such as those at Loughcrew and in the Boyne Valley, have smaller "satellite" cairns. A classic example is Knowth, near Newgrange, which is virtually ringed by smaller passage cairns. Moreover, in many cases the passages of these smaller mounds are directed towards the main site, as is the case at Knowth. It is not impossible to imagine, then, a kind of sonic web interlinking these places at times of ritual observance. Although we have no way of telling just how such a phenomenon as this acoustic site-hopping would have been understood, we can make an intelligent guess that it would have been imbued with magical or supernatural properties – perhaps viewed as the movement of the spirits from one site to another. It is, after all, a remarkable enough effect to hear even for us today, we who have an understanding of acoustic mechanics.

THE HELMHOLTZ RESONANCE

The final series of experiments at Camster Round revealed another type of acoustic phenomenon, one that – by virtue of a basic structural characteristic – potentially relates to all passage grave monuments: namely a narrow passage connecting to a spherical or rectangular chamber. This arrangement approximates that of a bottle with a narrow neck and relatively large body. If such a bottle, empty and uncorked, is held aloft in a stiff breeze or wind, a loud, hollow humming noise will be heard – a tone known as the Helmholtz resonance. This sound can also be produced to a lesser extent simply by blowing across the open neck of a bottle. It happens because the stream of air passing over the top of the bottle opening creates an edge-tone that sets up an oscillation of the air within the relatively constricted neck, which in turn interacts with the greater

< 99 >

volume of air in the body of the bottle to cause the sound of the wind passing the neck opening to become amplified.

While wind blowing past the (often exposed) entrance to a chambered mound's passageway might be able to induce Helmholtz resonance by stimulating the movement of air within the structure, this effect would probably be sporadic, and it is difficult to see how it could have been deliberately incorporated into a monument's overall scheme. But the interesting thing is that the effect can work in reverse: soundwaves generated in the chamber by an instrument like a drum cause the air within the chamber to expand and push at the block of air confined in the passage, which reacts as a single mass and is thrust outwards towards the entrance. Air, however, has an elastic quality and a point is reached where it recoils and sends the passage air back into the chamber. This to-and-fro movement is repeated until it synchronizes with the pressure of the soundwaves being produced by the source, causing these to increase in amplitude. The resulting amplification of the sound continues to be multiplied until it is greater than the original input, thereby generating a noise. "It is feasible that a megalithic tomb may be activated in this manner if the appropriate frequency of sound was introduced into the chamber," Watson has stated.[88]

At the university, Watson and Keating made a sophisticated three-dimensional model of Camster Round. By applying scaled soundwaves to it they were able to predict that the Helmholtz frequency there would be 4–6Hz – the silent sound of infrasound once again (see Chapters 3 and 4). It was also calculated that a single drum of 30 centimetres (12 inches) beaten within the chamber was capable of producing 4–5Hz at 120–130 decibels.

Back on site, the pair organized an experiment in which a drum was struck at four beats per second (hence 4Hz, and therefore able to excite Helmholtz resonance) inside the chamber with an audience present. People reported various subjective effects, and it was commonly noticed that pulse rates and breathing were being affected. If conditions were

< 100 >

maintained then hyperventilation was the likely result – one well-known method for inducing altered mind states. The Reading University investigators checked as far as was possible that it was the infrasound that was responsible rather than the audible components of the drumbeats. The investigators have written:

*"*Although the presence of infrasonics in sufficient quantities to influence people could not be absolutely confirmed, it was certainly apparent that the tomb interior was conducive to the creation of unusual experiences.*"* [89]

They went on to calculate the Helmholtz resonances of a number of other passage graves throughout the British Isles and Ireland. They ranged, variously, from 1Hz to 7Hz.

AN ORKNEY EXPEDITION

The two men's further acoustical enquiries took them to sites on Orkney, the group of islands off Scotland's northern coast. At the chambered mound of Maes Howe, whose inner stones are exceptionally well cut (dressed) and fitted, they found the Helmholtz resonance to be 2Hz. They also studied standing acoustic waves there, and found that a person moving in the passage caused fluctuations in the perceived sound in the chamber. As at Newgrange, the passage at Maes Howe has a blocking stone; this fits the entrance perfectly except for its height, for when in place it leaves a half-metre gap at the top. Lynch has suggested it served the same purpose as the Newgrange "roof-box". [90]

At the Stones of Stenness, a stone circle about 15 metres (49 feet) in diameter, distinctive acoustic effects were detected, notably echoes from the inner face of the stones that come together in a focused way at the geometric centre of the ring, where there is a large square stone setting of unknown purpose, referred to by archaeologists as a "hearth". Sound emitted from here returns simultaneously, whereas elsewhere in the ring the sound of the echoes is much less ordered.

There are two unusual chambered tombs on Orkney known as Huntersquoy and Taversoe Tuick. Each tomb has two chambers, one

< 101 >

on top of the other, with the solid stone floor of the top chamber dividing them. Each chamber is accessed by a separate passage from opposite sides of the mound, so two groups could have entered the mound independently and the occupants in one chamber could have heard sounds generated in the other. One archaeologist has pointed out that a miniature chamber set into the ground at the end of the passage at Taversoe Tuick could have been used to communicate with the lower chamber of the main tomb by speaking into the narrow aperture of its passage entrance.[91] Perhaps this was a more formal and complex oracle arrangement than the roof-boxes and apertures suggested by Lynch for Newgrange.

The investigators encountered the most dramatic acoustic effects of all at the Dwarfie Stane (see Plate 21), a sandstone rock 8.5 metres (28 feet) long, 4.2 metres (14 feet) high and 2.4 metres (8 feet) wide, with a passage and two chambers hewn out of its interior. The passage is 2.2 metres (7 feet) long but barely 0.7 metres (2 feet) high, and not much wider, while the chamber or cell is almost 2 metres (6 feet) wide and slightly higher than the passage. A block of stone found outside this rock-cut tomb was a closing stone for the passage entrance, but as at Maes Howe, and in keeping with Lynch's theory, this too would have left a narrow gap at the top when in place. Watson and Keating found it quite easy to use their voices to set up a resonant frequency. This sound developed a character of its own:

"When this happened, the sound appeared to become expansive and substantially fuller. At the same time, the massive stone block, and the air within it, appeared to shake vigorously. This vibration was also evident to listeners positioned outside the entrance and standing on the roof. Using sound in this way, one person can induce many tons of stones to appear to come alive in a manner which would be difficult to achieve by any other means."[92]

One idly wonders if the old folklore motif of moving and living megaliths may possibly have originated in such effects.

< 102 >

AND SO TO STONEHENGE ...

Among the sites to receive the more recent attentions of Watson and Keating has been Stonehenge, the most famous megalithic monument of them all. There, the two reprised their pink noise survey method, moving the microphone around the site between the stones to map out how sound behaved at the venerable holy place (see Plate 22). Watson referred to the way the stones of Stonehenge influenced the behaviour of sound as being "very dramatic".[93] As with the experience at Easter Aquorthies, there were places where sound was loud and other places where it was faint. Watson and Keating found sound to be at its clearest on the axis of the monument – the very line that points towards the famous midsummer sunrise position. "We wanted to test the idea that the sight line could also be a sound line," said Keating.[94] "The sound is very muffled around the back, but as you walk round it changes, and at the axis it is clearest." With their eyes closed, the investigators found they could tell exactly where they were in the great monument simply by using the echoes in the place.

The sarsen stones of Stonehenge (the larger stones at the site) were virtually all shaped in subtle ways, and this was achieved by the laborious method of hammering and grinding the great stones with stone balls (mauls, some of which have been found dumped at the site). The famous lintel stones across the uprights of the outer ring of Stonehenge are not simply straight blocks, but are instead slightly curved so that when they were all fitted together a perfect ring was formed. This lintel ring was also levelled – presumably by water troughs being used in the manner of spirit levels. So a degree of sophistication went into the construction of this mighty megalithic monument. It may have been even more sophisticated than archaeologists have hitherto suspected, if the observations of Watson and Keating are correct. They think that the inner surfaces of some of the upright sarsens, which have been subtly shaped so as to be slightly concave, may have been worked in this way order to focus sound at certain places (see Plate 23). For

< 103 >

example, the inner setting of giant sarsen stones is a horseshoe arrangement set on the monument's axis. The curved arc of stones was found to focus sound similar to the way that light can be focused by a parabolic mirror.

These observations may help explain the mystery of the stone settings known as "coves", which are found in other megalithic complexes. Most coves are three-sided arrangements of tall stone slabs, which form alcoves or open-sided "boxes", though the sites are now incomplete because various stones have fallen or disappeared. Coves are associated with some of the largest megalithic rings in western Europe, including England's Avebury and Stanton Drew, and Stenness in Orkney. (It is even possible that the horseshoe-shaped stone setting of Stonehenge is a variant form of cove.) The relationship between a cove and the stone ring is unclear – some coves may, in fact, have been free-standing features in existence before the stone circles were built. Prehistorian Aubrey Burl thinks they were transitional features between chambered tombs and stone circles, and that they developed from rectangular stone chambers in long burial mounds.[95] He suspects they were a focus for funerary rites, ones where there needed to be an audience, unlike the more secretive rites associated with the chambered mounds. The acoustic potential of coves is obvious: as Watson and Keating state, these features would have had the ability to project sound out in one direction while filtering it in others.

There are many more types of prehistoric site yet to be acoustically tested. For example, the two researchers Watson and Keating point out that open, earthwork monuments like henges are also suitable subjects for acoustic investigation – earth banks can also interrupt the passage of sound in controlled ways, just like earthen embankments are used today to act as sound baffles along major roads. The acoustic probing of prehistoric monuments looks set to continue. Who knows what we might yet overhear?

< 104 >

CHAPTER EIGHT

Talking Pictures

In addition to built monuments, acoustic researchers have made some initial investigations, using low- and high-tech methods, of *natural* sacred places of prehistory. The painted caves of the Old Stone Age – the Upper Palaeolithic, to be precise – have been targeted for research.

PAINTED CAVES

Palaeolithic cave paintings are to be found in southern France, Spain, Portugal and Italy, with a scattering in eastern Europe and Russia. Decorated bone and stone portable objects associated with finds of Ice Age animal bones and Palaeolithic stone tools were discovered in caves and rock-shelters in southwest France in the mid-nineteenth century, but the paintings on the cave walls were, incredibly, disregarded. In 1880, the archaeological establishment of the day rejected a suggestion made by a local amateur archaeologist that painted imagery discovered in the cave of Altamira in Spain was of prehistoric origin. Fifteen years later, wall paintings of bison were revealed at La Mouthe cave in the Dordogne after it had been cleared of fallen material containing Palaeolithic deposits. Eventually, the prehistoric origin of cave art could no longer be denied, and in the twentieth century many more sites were discovered, including the famous caves at Lascaux and Les Trois Frères in France, each of which contains hundreds of images. And painted caves continue to be uncovered – as recently as 1994 one of the most remarkable of them all, Chauvet, was found in France. In all, about 300 Palaeolithic painted cave sites are currently known.

Representational imagery in the caves consists mainly of animal forms. Many species are shown, though the most frequently depicted creatures are horses and bison, with mammoth and deer also fairly common – and there are some rhinos and lions. Images of composite animal-human figures have been noted at about fifteen cave sites, and it is thought that these show either were-creatures or shamans dressed in animal skins. The occurrence of human handprints or stencils is widespread throughout Palaeolithic cave art. (Mystery surrounds a number of these, because in caves sometimes hundreds of kilometres apart there are images made by hands with incomplete fingers, as if partially amputated.) However, the most common images to be found in Palaeolithic cave art are geometric markings. Called "signs" by archaeologists, these markings include dots, solid circles, lines, arcs, zigzags, rectangles and such-like. They can appear singly or in groups, sometimes associated with representational images or even superimposed on them.

In the main, cave paintings were made using black (manganese or charcoal) and red (iron oxide) pigments, applied by fingers and by spraying from the mouth or through a tube. Animal-hair brushes or softened, frayed twigs were also probably used. While many paintings were created on reasonably accessible walls, a number of them have been located deep within cave systems in places that are difficult to reach. Some painted panels are so high up on cave walls and cavern ceilings that scaffolding of some kind must have been used; indeed, holes that might have been made for such supports have been found. It certainly seems that the locations of the art had special significance – it was not some casual activity. Various dating techniques, including the radiocarbon dating of organic material such as the charcoal in pigments taken from the rock-surfaces, indicate that the paintings originate, variously, from between $c.30,000$ and $c.8000$BC. There is no evidence of any stylistic progression, with sophisticated examples dating from the earliest times. As well as paintings, there are a large number of engravings and high- and low-relief work in clay.

< 106 >

Theories about the meaning of cave art range from the now largely discredited idea that it is "hunting magic" to the more accepted notion that it is "trance-art", as has been found to be the case with prehistoric southern African San rock-art. It has been suggested that the "signs" are in fact "entoptic" markings resulting from trance states – these geometric mind patterns (like the jagged "fortification pattern" in migraine attacks) are universal – that is, they are common to the human nervous system and so can be expected to be found anywhere and in any time period that people used trance in their religious rites. Also, the human-animal hybrid figures on the cave walls could relate to body-image hallucinations known to be associated with altered mind states. The environment provided by these deep, ink-dark caves is itself profoundly conducive to the production of altered states of consciousness, with sensory deprivation being a key method of achieving such a condition, in addition to the use of drugs, chanting, dancing, fasting and other time-honoured ways of entering trance.

While some ideas remain controversial, most experts are nevertheless agreed that whatever went on in these caves tens of thousands of years ago was in some way associated with ritual activity. This is supported by finds such as that made in the Chauvet cave, where the first investigators to enter it found a bear skull that had been placed on a block of fallen stone all those millennia ago to give the appearance of an altar.

These ritual caves could well have been the natural prototypes of the chambers constructed within monumental, man-made mounds many centuries later (see Chapter 7). Like these chambers, the caves have noteworthy acoustic properties. "These caves are mostly resonant in themselves," French acoustic archaeologist Iégor Reznikoff has confirmed; "they are remarkable as acoustic pipes (that are also vaulted) and can produce quite astonishing echoing effects."[96]

Reznikoff and colleagues such as Michel Dauvois conducted their pioneering acoustic research in selected French painted caves between

< 107 >

1983 and 1985.[97] Aware of the powerful acoustic qualities in caves, and knowing that "there is no rite or celebration which does not use sound" and that the "more primitive the society, the greater the quality of sound perception", Reznikoff wanted to determine whether or not there was a relationship between the acoustics and the paintings in the caves.

The French investigators' research method was low-tech, involving tuning forks and the human voice, but Reznikoff was at pains to point out that human sound perception with a trained ear is of unequalled precision, and it also allows a flexibility of approach (one that proved invaluable for the work in hand). The procedure was simple but exact. The researchers would go through the different caverns or "galleries" of the selected caves and produce a range of vocal notes at regular spots, where they would listen for the resonance of the sounds along the cave walls in terms of intensity and duration. They particularly noted places where the quality of the resonance changed significantly. Resonance maps of the selected cave systems were then produced. These included the *pitch* of vocal sound that made the strongest resonance effect in a particular location. A location with a strong resonance effect was defined as one that displayed an increase in sound intensity of more than 15 decibels and which lasted for longer than two seconds or where the acoustic vibration extended for 25 metres (82 feet) or more.

After some practical experience, the researchers found that more or less any vocal sounds could be used, though an "mm" sound made with the mouth closed, or a more accentuated "hmm" sound, proved generally applicable. In some locations the production of the sound was sufficient to make up to 100 metres (328 feet) of a cave resound. "The voice is used quite minimally, since in a place of resonance a sound is immediately amplified," Reznikoff pointed out. "There is thus no need for a great intensity of sound. It is the cave's natural resonance alone that counts; a resonance created by the slightest vibration of a sound characteristic of the resonance and which will be amplified by the cave (or a part of the cave) if the frequencies correspond."[98]

< 108 >

WHISTLING IN THE DARK

The vocal sounds were produced spanning an almost three-octave register from middle C to G_3, extended for a further two octaves by strong harmonics, overtones and whistles. Upper harmonics of a sound were quickly dampened, but the fifth was found to be very important, and it was often this that helped the researchers locate the tonic (keynote). They walked through the caves, in the middle of a cavern or next to its walls, testing different sounds at different pitches. Eventually, at a certain pitch, the cave would respond. It was then necessary to ascertain the exact pitch that produced the resonance, whether there were other sounds (the fifth, for example) which responded, the precise location and orientation for achieving the best resonance (in terms of intensity and duration), and the exact point from where the resonance originated. Reznikoff describes the continuing process:

*"*One then continues along the path; the response might increase or decrease, might disappear or appear at a different pitch (there may be several pitches resounding at neighbouring points) and the special features must be particularly taken into account (recesses, alcoves). Those points where a new pitch is discovered, or where it reaches maximum intensity or duration are of course particularly notable; more generally one looks at points of maximum resonance, modified resonance, resonance related to another resonance (for example accompanied by a harmonic) or which is particularly distinctive.*"*[99]

The work varied in difficulty. In some places there was a dominant basic sound throughout most of a cavern, but in other caves there was what Reznikoff described as a "complex acoustic network", with resonances of different pitches in various places, resonances ranging from durations of over five seconds down to no resonance at all, and "from dull, lifeless resonance to the superb resonance of a chapel".

The voice was the chief acoustic tool used for the investigation because a drum has a fixed pitch and is not able to explore all the potential resonance points; flutes or whistles are too shrill to cause the

< 109 >

rock walls to resound; and percussive noises, such as feet-tapping, are too dull to work effectively. (Reznikoff remarked that this did not mean that such sounds were not used in support of the human voice in Palaeolithic rituals.)

Reznikoff reasoned that the Palaeolithic ritualists would have listened for the response of the cave, "which was doubtless considered alive", just as ringing rocks in Africa are considered as living things even today (see Chapter 9). Nor had the awe passed away with the ages: the French researchers found it striking to hear the deep echoes in the total darkness, and were extremely impressed on hearing "the cave reply from its very depths".

CAVERNS OF REVELATION

Reznikoff and his co-workers selected three caves in the Ariège Department in the French Pyrenees: Niaux, Fontanet and Le Portel. Work at Fontanet was inconclusive because it was found that an entry to the cave had been blocked by a landslide since prehistoric times, and this had irrevocably altered the resonance of the cavern system, which now had a uniform acoustic quality throughout. Niaux presented some practical research difficulties because of its size, while Le Portel proved to be the best site from a working point of view because the system has independent caverns or galleries: the Jeannel Gallery (Gallery 1), Jammes Gallery (Gallery 2), the Breuil, or Bison, Gallery and the Horse Gallery – some of the names referring to imagery found in them.

The French investigators did not expect to find a 100 percent match between the location of pictures and the points of main resonance. This was because not all the rock-surfaces were suitable for painting on, even if they resonated; in addition, allowance had to be made for the possibility that some of the reasons behind picture location may not have been due to acoustical considerations. Nevertheless, they obtained some startling statistics: in Niaux, nearly 90 percent of the cave paintings were found in the key resonant locations. There are a

< 110 >

multitude of possible locations for paintings in this cavern system, yet most of the pictures were found in places with the most remarkable acoustics. The cavern known as the Salon Noir was found to be "remarkably resonant" – and it was there that most of the paintings were located.

In Le Portel 80 percent of the paintings occurred in the chief resonant places. The main cavern or gallery, known as the Grande Salle, is not resonant and contains very few pictures (in notable contrast to the resonant Salon Noir in Niaux), but the acoustics team obtained remarkable results in some of the other galleries. In his papers, Reznikoff describes some of the correlations in detail, and one of the best examples of his findings involves the Jammes Gallery. As one enters this gallery, a red mark on the cave wall corresponds exactly to the occurrence of resonance A_1, a perfect fifth above D_1, the tonic of the gallery. The image of a small red horse on the opposite wall also marks this location. Continuing on through the gallery, the A is replaced by G just where several painted images, including horses, occur on the wall – the first large pictorial space after the red mark at the entrance. Yet further into the gallery there is a central resonant zone – an "essential sound node" as Reznikoff puts it – with resonances of D_1, A_1, D_2, E_2, but most in D_2 which, with D_1 and A_1, resounds with normal voice intensity to the end of the gallery 35 metres (115 feet) away in one direction, and as far back as the Horse Gallery, 70 metres (230 feet) away in the other. This central zone is marked by a figure described as having "a gnarled abdomen" and an erect penis. Further along, D_2 is dominant until it shifts to D_1, at which point there is a set of painted black signs. This resonance remains to the end of the gallery where it reaches its maximum intensity, at a cluster of more black signs. Standing at the end of the gallery and facing back along it, using the resonance D_1 (any other is quickly dampened), a vocal sound can be transmitted as far away as an owl image at the entrance to the gallery, some 100 metres (328 feet) distant. In summary, the key resonant places in the Jammes

< 111 >

Gallery are also the exact locations where wall paintings occur. Reznikoff suspected that the red sign was "of purely acoustic significance".

There was thus a notable complete match between images and sounds in the Jammes Gallery, and in general in their overall research Reznikoff and colleagues found such a high degree of correlation that they concluded that "the location for a rock painting was chosen to a large extent because of its sound value".[100] So confident were they of this conclusion, that they literally blind-tested it in some experiments: they advanced in pitch darkness and identified strong points of resonance; on illuminating those places, painted imagery was confirmed to be present at them. Another conclusion was that because of the relatively low resonances involved, "it was men's voices that were used" in Palaeolithic times, foreshadowing the findings of the ICRL team at the Neolithic chambered mounds (see Chapter 7). Reznikoff stressed that this did not necessarily mean that women were not involved in the rituals, but simply that men led the chanting or singing, or used their voices to seek the magical or spirit-haunted resonant places for the paintings.

In later, higher-tech work Reznikoff and Dauvois conducted tests at Le Portel in which wide-band sound signals with flat output characteristics were broadcast and the results measured and analysed at a variety of locations. The results similarly convinced Dauvois that the occupation, utilization and decoration of particular parts of such caves, from whole galleries down to niches, had been influenced by a fascination with acoustic effects. Some of the acoustic "hot spots" even appear to have been marked in prehistoric times by patterns of dots applied to the cave walls.[101]

The French investigators also encountered some curious special effects during their acoustical mapping work. At the exceptionally decorated Camerin double recess in Le Portel's Breuil Gallery, the sound of exhaling was found to be enough to set up a resonant reaction or, at least, a sense of vibration felt in the head. On vocal emission,

< 112 >

sounds that resembled "a growl or the lowering of a bison" were sent resounding down the whole gallery. As Reznikoff commented, it is inconceivable that a Stone Age cave painter would have failed to notice these effects.

It was just such effects that attracted another researcher, the American Steven Waller, who introduced more high-tech methods to the acoustical study of the Palaeolithic painted caves.

IN SEARCH OF "SOUNDTRACKS"

Waller had become aware of minor references to acoustics in the rock-art literature – comments such as there being "acoustic space" in caverns, or rock-art sites having echoes at them as a "phenomenal attribute" – and he had read some of the papers by Reznikoff, Dauvois and their colleagues, but it was a personal experience in 1987 that really fired his interest. Waller was standing outside the mouth of a painted cave in France when he became struck by the psychological power of echoes "'mysteriously' emanating from the cave in answer to sounds made outside".[102] He realized that in the period preceding the modern scientific understanding of acoustics, echoes and reverberation phenomena would have been thought of as being "spontaneously generated noises" that would have bestowed "a magic aura to such locations as caves and canyons that reflect sound".

Waller carried out some experiments by making different kinds of noises in a variety of acoustic environments. He discovered that when rocks are struck together in the manner of one making stone tools, "the echoes sound remarkably like the hoof beats of galloping horses".[103] He learned that a majority of the animal figures depicted in Palaeolithic rock-art were of hoofed animals, as well as creatures such as mammoths with hard, pounding feet, so he decided to test the acoustic responses to percussive effects in places where such rock-art existed.

The method employed by Waller involved the making of a given set of single, loud, percussive sounds – striking rocks, clapping hands, yelling in

< 113 >

a sharp vocal burst and using a spring-loaded device capable of making a percussive sound of reproducible intensity at a level comparable to natural clapping. After the generation of each single percussive sound, the direction was noted from which the resulting reflected sound was heard, and it was subjectively judged for its characteristics. In addition, acoustic equipment was deployed for quantitative testing – a high-quality tape recorder and microphone, and precision sound-level meters. During the on-site recordings the same positioning of the recording equipment relative to the original sound source was maintained at all the locations. Playback of the recordings was by means of an auditorium sound system, through which the primary percussive burst, the subsequent reflected sound and the background ambient noise of each site were isolated and measured separately.

Waller sampled a selection of cave sites in France. As a general pattern, he found that echoes vibrate at an average level of 3 decibels in the caves, but rock-art panels of hoofed animals produce reflected sound of 23–31 decibels. Panels showing feline creatures, on the other hand, average a much lower 1–7 decibels. Unpainted surfaces tended to be "totally flat".[104] "Carnivores were observed to be associated with the disappearance of sound reflection in the interior of the caves," Waller expanded.[105]

At the Font de Gaume cavern, the galleries where images of hoofed beasts are concentrated all gave the strongest and longest duration vibrations in the whole cave system. A terminal fissure containing the image of a feline creature yielded, in comparison, a statistically significant decrease in sound reflection. The Chamber of the Bulls at Lascaux – where there are evenly spaced and balanced rock-paintings of large bulls – produces deep, long-lasting sounds coming from all directions. At the location known as the Nave, where there are paintings of two back-to-back, mirror-image bison, Waller found echoes to be stereophonically identical in each direction. In Lascaux's Chamber of Felines, though, there was an almost complete lack of sound reflection, because it has sound-absorbent soft clay walls. In a sound-amplifying

< 114 >

hollow in the cavern system of Les Combarelles he found a painting of a human being apparently clapping hands, and the most intense reverberations were found at the greatest concentration of hoofed animal depictions. At Bernifal, Waller encountered a sound of great intensity emanating from a side-tunnel that contained drawings of mammoths. In La Mouthe the majority of the art, which includes mammoths and bison, proved to be in the chambers with the most powerful acoustics. In the cave of Cougnac the final chamber has "magnificent, very profound reverberations of unusually long duration".[106] At the entrance to this chamber there are paintings of hoofed animals on a concave wall – the precise location from which the reflected sound appears to originate. The American investigator found that at other locations within this chamber – for example, at symbols directly opposite the painted walls – the sound still seems to emanate from where the animals are painted. In Rouffignac's Chamber of the Hundred Mammoths there are numerous examples of mirror-image mammoths confronting or facing one another, and in each case Waller once more recorded stereophonically symmetrical sound reflection. The Painted Ceiling in Rouffignac, with its concentration of mammoths, horses and ibexes, was found to positively "buzz" with a flutter echo. Waller considered that the strong acoustics at this spot were due to a deep pit located directly underneath the stone ceiling.

"Modern humans, who understand sound reflection, tend to trivialize echoes, and this may be the reason why the motivation for rock-art has remained so long an enigma," Waller concluded, recalling the anthropological case of traditional Pacific Islanders who revere echoes because they believe that an echo, as a bodiless voice, is the earliest of all existence. To the Palaeolithic ear, the echoes in the caves must have seemed like the sounds of invisible, spirit creatures. "The discovery that echoes of percussive noises resemble to a remarkable degree the sounds of galloping hoofed animals provides a crucial link between the context and the content of the art."[107]

< 115 >

DISTANT ECHOES

Waller's quest for the "soundtracks" to prehistoric pictures has taken him further afield than France (see Plate 24). He encountered some different and remarkable acoustic effects in Australia, where ancient Aboriginal rock-art is typically painted on the curved walls of rock-shelters (see Plate 25). When he placed himself about 30 metres (98 feet) from an Aboriginal painted wall, echoes seemed to emanate from the central images, but when he made noise closer in to the wall, it reflected back too quickly to be distinguished from the original sound. It was "almost spooky" Waller admitted. "Where they've drawn a person, and you yell at it, it's like the person is speaking to you."[108] This highly specialized acoustic effect is due to the curved rock-walls acting in a similar way to a parabolic mirror focusing light. (Ancient North American Indian rock-art has also come within Waller's research remit, but that is described in Chapter 10.)

OUT IN THE OPEN

In addition to the cave art of the Palaeolithic age, there is open-air rock-art of that era and also of the Neolithic period, and both Reznikoff and Waller have made some preliminary acoustic investigations of it. In addition to similar studies made in the United States, Waller conducted some tests at Palaeolithic open-air rock-art sites in France (where some of the rock-art has been removed to museums to safeguard against further weather erosion and potential vandalism). At the Rock Shelter of the Sorcerers, Angles-sur-l'Anglin, he found that when he stood on a slope across the stream from the site, two or three strong echoes emanated precisely from the rock-shelter where the images of hoofed animals were originally located. "The powerful echo intensity from that place is due to the wave-focusing effect of both the shelter and the concave shape of the surrounding cliff face itself," Waller observed.[109] He learned that at Vallon des Roches, which contains several rock-art sites, it has been found that in the winter, when foliage is scant, powerful echoes have been clearly heard during demonstrations of stone tool-making techniques given by the site guides. A bizarre echo phenomenon occurs in the Vallée de la Grande Beune, which has the rock-art sites of Commarque, Laussel and Cap Blanc (noted for its life-sized bas-reliefs of horses and bison). A sound produced in the valley creates distinct echoes that come in a series from the various mountainsides, giving the impression that the source of the sound moves. At Oreille d'Enfer (Ear of Hell), Waller discovered that a sound creates an echo from a facing cliff at the head of the gorge. Positioning himself at that cliff, he found that the source of the echo was the spot where deep engravings of hoofed animals were located. Waller went on to find that the small canyons outside the painted caves of Font de Gaume, La Mouthe and Les Combarelles/Grotte Rey all produce clear multiple echoes. These can be heard either at the cave entrances, or at positions across the canyons, when the echoes appear to come from the mouth of the caves.

In 1987 Reznikoff looked at examples of Neolithic open-air rock-art sites in Finland – around three lakes near Helsinki and one in the area of Mikkeli. The rock-art at these sites has been tentatively dated to between 3500 and 2000BC. This time, "a powerful singing technique" was used, from D_2 to D_3 and 100–110 decibels at source, in front of each of the sites, and facing whatever the associated lake was in the Helsinki samples.[110] The basic criterion was to establish if the site coincided with a location presenting exceptional echo effects – the researchers' minimum requirement was a triple echo. In the Helsinki area they first tested a site almost on the shore of Nuuksionjärvi (the actual Swan Lake). The rock has a pictograph (painting) on it depicting an elk. The location produced three echoes, while areas around it produced only two. On the eastern edge of Lake Vitträsk, at Valkoinen-järvi (White Lake), paintings of a reindeer and geometric signs were discovered in 1917 in a recess on a cliff about 15 metres (49 feet) above the water's surface. The site yielded three good echoes, and Reznikoff felt that without the wind that was blowing on the day of the test, more would have been heard. Places around the site, above and below it on the cliff, produced less clear echoes. A pictograph site at Juusjärvi, discovered in 1963, has images of some human figures, a

< 117 >

hand, a fish and zigzag lines. They are located about 5 metres (16 feet) above the water on the southeastern edge of the lake – and the position proved remarkable as regards echoes, yielding four echoes, with the last being an echo of an echo. A site on Lake Yöveşi near Mikkeli did not produce good results, but it was learned that the water level had been lowered by several metres since prehistoric times. This obviously affected the acoustics of the rock-art site, because the surface of the water is an excellent propagator of soundwaves. This prompted Reznikoff to comment that discovering the level of the water surface at the time that waterside prehistoric rock-art was created should be seen as a key element in establishing the full siting characteristics of such places.

Reznikoff observed that the best acoustic effects at the sites were obtained when actually on the surface of the lake – the initiating vocal sound being projected from a boat. This would fit in well with what is known of Scandinavian prehistoric societies up to and including Viking times, when boats played a tremendously important ritual role as well as a practical one. He also noted that the old Finnish epics indicated that the practice of echo effects was common in ancient Finland, especially on the lakes, and that it survived until the nineteenth century.

While most places produce no or only minimal echo effects, many places do, so the brief sampling represented by this kind of research can, of course, be seen only as suggesting an acoustic connection with outdoor rock-art sites rather than proving one. Reznikoff was fully aware of this, naturally, and called for a detailed analysis of the acoustics of such sites in a particular area – a set of Finnish lakes would be a good case study. It would be a huge undertaking, however, with hundreds of sites needing to be tested and further research required to determine whether conditions around them today more or less matched those when the art was created. Until such large-scale research is carried out, work like Reznikoff's has to serve to alert us to the possibility that there was an acoustic dimension to prehistoric rock-art, whether it is found inside caves or out in the open.

< 118 >

CHAPTER NINE

Stone Age Rock 'n' Roll

Most of the current acoustic archaeological research centres on the real-time production of sound at ancient sites and interpreting the resulting effects. But is it possible to actually hear what Stone Age people heard? Or, to put it another way, have ancient sounds been "fossilized"? There are strands of acoustical inquiry that, fortunately, are able to provide positive answers to those questions.

RINGING ROCKS

The most basic of Stone Age musical sounds were extracted by (usually) percussive means from the natural environment in the form of "ringing rocks". These are naturally occurring rocks and stones that produce bell- or drum-like sounds when struck. Examples of the ancient usage of such fascinating rocks are known of in the British Isles, Brittany, Portugal, Nigeria, Cameroon, Uganda, the Sudan and Asia (they were also used by American Indians; see Chapter 10) . Evidence of their ancient usage is usually found in the form of "chatter marks" or "cupules" – small, cup-like depressions created by repeated and carefully aimed striking of the rock's surface with a hammerstone. Such rocks could produce sounds simply in their unaltered form, or else their effects were enhanced by such subtle engineering techniques as the raising of one edge of a rock by means of packing it with small stones. There are also examples of segments of naturally ringing rocks being removed to provide portable or resituated versions.

In Britain "ringing rocks" may conceivably provide part of the answer to one of the enduring mysteries of archaeology – the presence of the bluestones at Stonehenge (the smaller stones at the site – one of which can be seen standing behind the microphone on the tripod in Plate 22), which came from the Preseli Hills in southwest Wales. Much intellectual energy has been expended arguing *how* they travelled the approximately 320 kilometres (200 miles) to Stonehenge, whether carried by glacial action or human effort, and some physical energy has been expended trying to demonstrate that the latter was at least feasible. Less energy has been expended in trying to figure out *why* the bluestones should have been such revered objects, for such they were – being used for the first stone setting on the Stonehenge site, and various arrangements of them were made before the erection of the larger sarsen uprights and lintels most people associate with the image of Stonehenge today. There was a Stone Age tradition of taking rocks and clays from one area and depositing them at another, something that has been interpreted as the circulation of "pieces of places" – as if to transfer the charisma of one sacred place to another, in some cases from a venerated natural place to a built monument.[111] The practice is somewhat akin to the medieval Christian one of circulating the relics of saints. Bernard Fagg, a scholar generally credited with raising awareness of ringing rocks in the 1950s, reported that his investigations of the Preseli Hills had resulted in the discovery of many excellent ringing rocks. "It is probable that the exceptional sanctity of the Prescelly Mountains [sic] ... was due in some measure to the ringing quality of so many of its rocks," Fagg suggested.[112] Indeed, there is a village called Maenclochog ("Ringing Rocks") situated at the feet of the Preseli. It was so named because of two rock-gongs in its vicinity, but these were destroyed for use as roadbuilding material in the late eighteenth century. Even up until recently, though, there has been local attention paid to the phenomenon of "anathoths" – open-air places where echoes can be heard. These have been discovered close to standing stones, particularly in hilly areas like the Preseli.[113]

While exploring the concentration of megalithic monuments in the Carnac region of Brittany, Fagg noted that a number of the horizontal

< 120 >

slabs of rocks on the dolmens there issued "a bell note when struck, and also had suggestive though inconclusive signs of wear". He additionally found that the giant fallen Breton megalith of Er Grah at Locmariaquer "had a voice", as he put it. Weighing 342 tons, this great megalith – now broken into four fragments: three smaller and one larger – had stood 20 metres (66 feet) tall when it was erect. This made it the tallest known standing stone in Europe (see Plate 26). It is of a non-local granite and the transportation of such a huge block must have been a mighty undertaking – a task that obviously had some underlying purpose. Its importance may have been because it was a ringing rock. When visiting the huge monolith, Fagg was instructed by a local man to place his ear at one end of the longest segment while the man struck the opposite end with a stone. This caused it to issue a ringing sound (reminiscent of the granite obelisk at Karnak; see Chapter 6).

Elsewhere in Brittany there is a small rock-gong at the cave-shrine of St Gildas at Castennec, near Pontivy. Fagg remarked that it was presently placed upside down on a recently built pedestal. The original, deeply worn, percussion surface is thus underneath, but its exceptional wearing indicates an exceedingly long period of use. It may well be a prehistoric feature that has been Christianized, in the same way that several of the major megalithic monuments of Brittany were Christianized by the addition of crosses.

Fagg was based at a museum in Nigeria, and reported on a number of ringing rocks in that country. For example, he drew attention to a group of rock-gongs at Dutsen Murufu near Birnin Kudu, in northern Nigeria's Kano Province. These rocks are close to prehistoric cave paintings and a "rock slide" – literally a slippery and worn strip of rock-slope that locals used for sliding down. It is highly likely that such slides had a ritual significance for earlier peoples, because they are found elsewhere to be associated with rock-art sites – Fagg himself mentioned a slide found by rock-carvings (petroglyphs) near Lusaka in Zambia. Folklore relating to five rock-slides in Brittany associated them

< 121 >

with old pagan fertility rites – hinting at an earlier ritual usage there. "Rock slides and rock gongs seem likely to occur in most parts of Africa and in many other parts of the world," Fagg remarked. "It may be that an intensive study of their occurrence and association with paintings and petroglyphs may significantly assist in the interpretation of prehistoric cave art."[114] This prescient idea was later underscored by James Vaughan, who studied the contemporary usage of rock-gongs by the Marghi of Nigeria, and found that they were employed in rites of passage. He felt that more ethnological enquiries of this kind "may lead to new discoveries of paintings, gongs and associated phenomena".[115]

"Sounding stones" are also known in southeast Asia. For example, Danish researcher Erik Seidenfaden noted a flat piece of rock in Bangkok's National Museum which issues a bell-like note when it is struck with a hard object.[116] Such pieces of ringing rocks were used in ancient Thailand instead of bells. Even older were the ten sounding stones discovered in 1949 in Vietnam: they were oblong-shaped and had been cut out of the living rock – the heaviest piece weighed about 3 kilograms (more than 6 pounds). The pieces were thought to date to a Neolithic culture that occupied the region thousands of years ago, and they had probably formed "a kind of xylophone, giving a whole scale of notes", Seidenfaden ventured.

NORTHERN ROCK MUSIC

The Karetski Peninsula is on the eastern shore of Lake Onega, the second largest lake in Europe, which is situated north of St Petersburg in Karelskaya, a part of Russia relatively close to the Finnish border. About 150 petroglyphs are carved on the coastal rocks there and are thought to date to the Neolithic era. Amid this rock-art is what Russian and Scandinavian researchers refer to as a "palaeoacoustic site". It is a stone "drum" consisting of a thick slab of rock lying at an angle across a natural fissure that runs for 10 metres (33 feet) down to the waters of the lake. When struck with a stick, the stone slab resonates with a very

< 122 >

low bass sound. Experiments have shown that on calm summer days this deep tone can be heard right across the peninsula – a distance of some 4 kilometres (2.5 miles). The low pitch means that the soundwaves are long, thus enabling them to travel considerable distances, but there seems to be a natural amplification system at work too. "The crack acts like a cable – it conducts sounds to the lake and on the surface of the water," says Finnish rock-art researcher, Rauno Lauhakangas.[117] The soundwaves from the drum apparently reverberate down the fissure ensuring that most of the energy is transferred to the surface of the lake, which then acts like a vast loudspeaker.

There is no rock-art actually on the drum, but examples occur all around it, with the nearest petroglyph lying 10 metres (33 feet) from it. One of the Karetski petroglyphs depicts a snake, which is carved on a rock so close to the water's surface that waves can flow along it, sluicing through its deeply engraved lines. The sun glints on this channelled water to create the illusion that the snake is actually moving. Lauhakangas wonders if this is a reference to the stone drum, in that snakes are very sensitive to ground vibrations, which can, of course, be caused by deep bass notes.

While the stone drum has been known about for some time, researchers have recently discovered two more palaeoacoustic sites on the east shore of the lake, one of which has been described as a "singing rock". Field studies are continuing – a slow process because of the remoteness of the lake and the fact that it is ice- and snowbound for the duration of the long winter months. The existence of acoustic features around the lake might be expected, though, if note is taken of the lake's Finnish name – Aänijärvi, which means "Sound Lake".

The evidence for the Onega stone drum being a natural artefact that was deliberately used in Neolithic times for its acoustic properties is circumstantial, though compelling. A journey even further back in time is required for what amounts virtually to proof of the acoustic use of natural features in prehistoric Europe, curiously enough to the Palaeolithic era.

< 123 >

ROCKS OF AGES

During his investigations in France, Bernard Fagg visited the Cougnac cave in the Dordogne. He was "very impressed by the infinite variety of 'metallic' notes which could be produced by tapping the stalactites with a pebble".[118] Near some of the cave paintings he further noted the presence of horizontal fragments of stalactites exhibiting vertical calcite accretions, signifying that they had been broken in ancient times – "perhaps by the men who made the paintings".

These observations by Fagg presaged what was to become a significant line of inquiry into Stone Age acoustics. In the 1960s a French priest, who exulted in the surname of Glory, drew attention to musical stalactites in the painted caves of France and the Iberian peninsula, and in the 1980s the Belgian archaeologist Lya Dams conducted a detailed study of such features, which came to be called "lithophones".

Dams's starting point was the Spanish cave system of Nerja, not far from Malaga. The caverns there are lofty with excellent acoustics, and occupation deposits have been unearthed there dating back to *c.*10,000BC. At the time of her investigation, nineteen paintings had been recorded within the cave, but she went on to itemize some 500 other figures, the majority of them painted markings or images in red or black, and a few engravings. Animal figures are scarce, and most markings consist of abstract symbols and signs. Nerja's lithophone is called "the Organ" and is a recess or "sanctuary" consisting of a triangular platform with a steep bank on one side and, on the other, a wall of tightly packed fluted calcite folds or "draperies" some 5 metres (16 feet) in length and 4 metres (13 feet) in height (see Plate 27). These calcite folds have been tilted at an angle of 45 degrees due to earthquake activity in the past. To reach this feature, the users of the cave during the Stone Age would have to have climbed over several huge boulders from the bottom of the main cavern, from which the Organ is not visible. An abstract sign, which Dams called the "Beckoning Sign", is found on a stalagmitic pillar on the approach to the Organ recess – and it is the only sign that can be

< 124 >

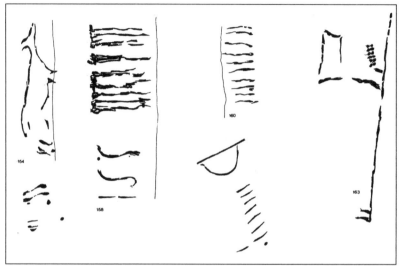

Fig. 8. Some of the markings on the Nerja lithophone. Note the climbing hind on the left side. (L. Dams, 1984)

seen from any sort of distance. Various sounds can be elicited from the calcite folds when their edges are struck with a hard object. Dams's team experimented with blunt flints and wooden sticks, the latter working best, to produce clear, harp-like notes which reverberated to the rear of the cave.[119] It was noted that several of the calcite edges had been intentionally broken at various heights in ancient times – probably to vary the sounds. The edges of the folds have a worn appearance, indicating percussive usage over a considerable time period.

The Organ is both visually and acoustically impressive. Dams's examination of the feature confirmed earlier claims by Glory that there were paintings on it – many tucked away in the grooves between the folds. There were dozens of signs and markings – dots, strokes, spirals – and a small number of representational images including a hind seemingly climbing up one of the drapes (see Figure 8). It was clear that

< 125 >

these paintings in red and black were not meant for display, but were more likely to have been adornments of a feature to which the cave's users had obviously attached great importance, for the cave-artists did their work at this place without regard to visibility or easy access. Some of the markings start at a height in excess of 2 metres (over 6 feet) from the ground, and when she was recording them Dams found herself using artificial toeholds to reach the images, holes that must have been made by the original artists. Close examination revealed that some of the red signs had been overpainted long ago.

Later, Dams turned her attention to some of the French caves that had been identified by Glory as having lithophones. The Roucadour cave at Thémines consists of a succession of caverns, or "halls", ending in a small subterranean lake. In 1961, a lateral gallery was discovered, its narrow entrance having been obscured by great blocks of rock. It contains a frieze of painted and engraved bisons, horses, a mammoth, stencilled hands, circular symbols and other signs. All of them are positioned in a narrow cleft some 6 metres (19 feet) from the floor of the gallery. Glory discovered that a wall of the cleft had long ago been bombarded with large clay pellets. He felt this "rite" had been "accompanied by rhythmic sounds", because nearly 7 metres (23 feet) to the right of the clay balls was a stalagmitic fall, the folds of which had been broken in ancient times at human-height, while the upper and lower folds were untouched. The stalagmitic feature was marked by two black dots. Dams found the decorated gallery to be large enough to have accommodated between twenty and thirty people. The walls were all even enough for paintings, yet only the cleft had been decorated. The lithophone is located on the right-hand side of the entrance, preceding the cleft; it consists of an impressive fall of several layers of tightly packed folds, many of which had been broken in earlier times (see Plate 28). Soot marks, presumably from a smoking torch in prehistoric times, smudge some of the folds. In one area of the feature, broken-off pieces of calcite had been wedged back into a fold, where

< 126 >

they are now cemented by a layer of calcite, thus indicating the antiquity of their placing (see Plate 29). In addition to the black painted dots Glory mentioned, Dams discovered two small "branch-like" signs. She also found that to the right of these was a long stalactite that "gives out a very pure, bell-like sound".[120]

Another cave examined by Dams was Cougnac, near Gourdon, which consists of a main cavern with two smaller "halls". Most of the art is concentrated in the main cavern, while some narrow passages contain signs and symbols. Glory had remarked on stalactites here that emit "crystalline sounds when they are struck with, preferably, a wooden rod", but he did not exactly specify where they were located, so Dams had to hunt them out. She found a small group of broken stalactites which when struck emit high and clear vibrations which can be heard over a considerable distance through the cave. They are covered with a thick layer of calcite through which some red ochre dots and strokes can be discerned. The second lithophone at Cougnac was found to consist of a large stalagmite, broken at a height of just over a metre (4 feet). "Its scarred and worn appearance points to repeated use on both faces," Dams remarked. "It emits a deep, muffled but resonant sound comparable to a gong."[121] Traces of red and black markings could be made out through the thick layer of calcite covering both faces of the truncated stalagmite (see Figure 9). A cup-like marking on the front of the feature was reminiscent of a navel, Dams thought, and it had been enhanced by red paint. Dams's detective work uncovered a third lithophone at Cougnac: it was an overhang of smooth calcite framed by fringes of stalactites at top and bottom. Showing through a calcite layer, black and red images are painted on the smooth surface. They consist of a faint antler image, an animal that possibly represents a wolf, and three truly curious anthropomorphic figures that have been nicknamed "phantoms" (see Plate 30). They are partial figures, outlined in black. One figure has been painted over a previous red outline and has stumpy outstretched arms, and its trunk is outlined by dots. The

< 127 >

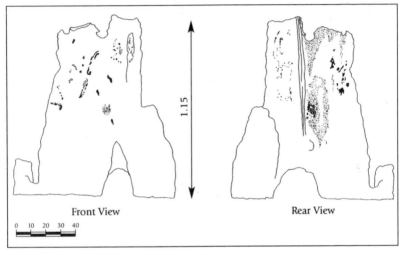

Front View   Rear View

0 10 20 30 40

Fig. 9. Markings on both faces of the second lithophone at Cougnac:
black = black markings; dotted grey = red markings. (L. Dams, 1985)

stalactites constituting a lower fringe have been chipped and broken in
many places, and give forth "pure and clear vibrations" when beaten,
according to Dams.

Dams went on to explore the spectacular Pech Merle cave at
Cabrerets, famed for its paintings of spotted horses and the so-called
"Chapel of the Mammoths". The lithophone here is in the form of a
calcite disk 1 metre (about 3 feet) across. It is located at the rear of a
large chamber, far from the decorated caverns and at the end of a gallery
containing the engraved head of a bear. It can be seen from a ledge
containing ancient (calcified) footprints, but access is difficult through
a low and narrow corridor. The disk is in a vertical position, naturally
cemented to a kind of stalagmitic pedestal. It yields a gong-like sound.

A fourth French cave on Dams's research itinerary was Les Fieux at
Miers. It was discovered in 1964, and a mass of archaeological deposits
was found within it, dating from the Neolithic back to the Middle

< 128 >

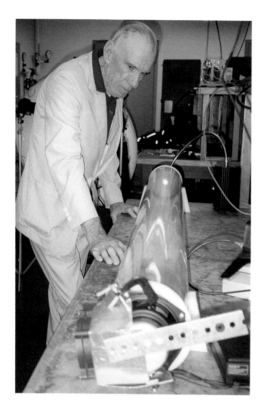

17. Professor Robert G. Jahn with the experimental set-up at Princeton University designed to check the potential role of the Newgrange passage as a functioning Kunst tube – a device used in physics experiments for revealing visibly the pattern of soundwaves (Chapter 7). (Arnold Lettieri)

18. The recumbent stone and associated stones in the Easter Aquorthies stone circle, Scotland. This is the place in the circle where acoustic research indicates a ritual officiant would have stood (Chapter 7).

19. *Camster Round passage grave, Scotland, with Camster Long in the distance. It was found that drumming inside one site could be heard inside the other (Chapter 7). (Aaron Watson)*

20. *Acoustic archaeologist Aaron Watson taking measurements inside the passage in Camster Round (Chapter 7). (Aaron Watson)*

21. *The Dwarfie Stane, Orkney, Scotland. This Neolithic rock-hewn chamber gave the illusion of moving when appropriate sound frequencies were generated within it (Chapter 7). The passage blocking stone can be seen in the foreground.* (Aaron Watson)

22. *Acoustic investigators David Keating (left) and Aaron Watson (right) with some of their equipment in the centre of Stonehenge (Chapter 7).*

23. The inner faces of the sarsen stones at Stonehenge have been made slightly concave, as careful inspection reveals in these examples (Chapter 7). The better to direct and focus ritual sounds?

24. Acoustician Steven Waller pictured alongside prehistoric American Indian rock art (Chapters 8 and 10). (Steven Waller)

25. *Typical location for ancient Australian Aboriginal rock-art – a rock shelter with curved walls, which can act to focus echoes on particular images (Chapter 8). A nearby boulder is covered in cupules, indicating that it may have been struck to produce percussive sounds to create echoes. This example is in Western Australia.*

26. *The great fallen standing stone of Er Grah, Brittany, France. Its longest fragment rings like a bell when struck (Chapter 9).*

27. A formation of naturally musical calcite folds on the side of a recess known as "the Organ" in the Spanish cave of Nerja, near Malaga (Chapter 9). (Lya Dams)

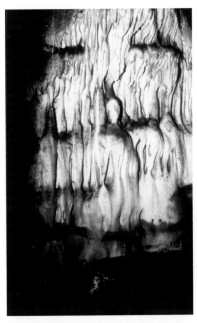

28. A musical stalagmitic fall in the cave of Roucadour, France (Chapter 9). (Jean Vertut)

29. These fallen fragments of the Roucador musical stalagmite were pressed back into one of its fissures in prehistoric times, indicating the veneration in which the natural lithophone must have been held (Chapter 9). (Jean Vertut)

30. *The third lithophone at the Cougnac Cave, France (Chapter 9). The stalactites near the bottom of this panel are musical. Note the rock art figures, nicknamed "phantoms". (Jean Vertut)*

31. *The lithophone at the Les Fieux cave, France. (Jean Vertut)*

32. *Giant fused stalactites/stalagmites in the Mayan ritual cave of Lol-Tun, Yucatán, Mexico. They issue a deep tone when struck (Chapter 10).*

33. *A few of the phalli stones at Chichén Itzá, Yucatán, Mexico. Certain ones of these are said to issue ringing sounds when struck with a wooden mallet (Chapter 10).*

35. *Making a digital audio recording of the Castillo's strange birdcall echo. This location by the Temple of Venus is the specific spot from where the effect can best be created (Chapter 10).*

34. *The Castillo, the temple of the Feathered Serpent, Kukulcan, at Chichén Itzá. At the bottom of each balustrade there is the carving of a serpent's head. This monument seems to be the seat of both visual and acoustic symbolism (Chapter 10).*

Palaeolithic – the cave had clearly been a favoured place in prehistory. The cave art consists of engravings, a few paintings and stencilled hands. The lithophone is a stalagmitic mass located at the centre of the main cavern (see Plate 31). With the unsealing of Les Fieux having been so recent, Glory was able to assert with confidence that the fractures on it were of Palaeolithic origin – they had recalcified, like those at Cougnac and Roucadour. Because of its central location, and obvious use, Glory felt that it must have played a part in ritual ceremonies. Dams describes it as being about 2 metres (6 feet) tall. It is undecorated (though it is near a block that has an engraved ibex, cup marks and other engravings, including one of a mammoth) and produces a resonant sound like a gong.

Dams followed the Glory trail to Portugal. There, the relatively small, winding cave of Escoural, at Santiago do Escoural, is the only Portuguese cave so far discovered that contains Palaeolithic art.[122] It has many engravings and paintings in black and red. The lithophone is a stalagmitic canopy formed by a thick flow of calcite over a sloping stone block. There are calcite pendants and folds, which when struck with a wooden rod produce "sonorous vibrations" as Glory described it. The folds were chipped in ancient times. The feature is the focus of much rock-art, including two human figures – one with a bird's head, the other with that of a horse. There are also partial outlines of quadrupeds, as well as a range of abstract signs. To have painted these images, Dams proposed that the artist would have endured a most uncomfortable cramped posture, despite there being smooth, even wall surfaces nearby that were much more accessibly located. She saw this as yet again evidence of the acoustic properties of the lithophone presenting powerful motivation to the cave-artists.

The cave lithophones show beyond any reasonable doubt that people as far back as the Palaeolithic era did create sounds, consciously and deliberately, and revered the places where those noises emerged. The chipping and breaking of the calcite folds on them was a way of

< 129 >

Fig. 10. Musical notation of some of the lithophone sounds: Roucadour (top); third lithophone, Cougnac (second from top); Escoural (second from bottom); Nerja (bottom). (L. Dams, 1985)

controlling the pitch of the sounds produced (the shorter the fold, the higher the pitch, and vice versa), raising the question of planned melody – Dams made musical notation of the sounds produced by the various lithophones (see Figure 10). A number of investigators, Glory, Reznikoff and Dauvois among them, suspect that lithophones are related to cave depictions of animals – the correlation is "too close and recurrent to be merely coincidental".[123]

< 130 >

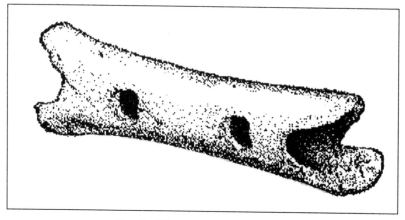

Fig. 11. The Divje Babe "bone flute"

STONE AGE SYMPHONIES

The final plank of evidence proving the existence of a developed acoustic sense in Stone Age Europeans is provided by the discovery of musical instruments in Palaeolithic caves. Just how far back this sense goes, though, is still a contentious matter among scholars.

What may be the oldest musical instrument yet to be found in Europe is the supposed flute discovered in 1995 at the Divje Babe cave in Slovenia by archaeologist Ivan Turk and colleagues (see Figure 11). It was excavated in association with material that indicated Neanderthal occupation of the cave some 40,000 years ago. The instrument, if such it be, is part of the hollow thigh bone of a young bear, and it possesses two complete and two partial holes like finger-holes on a flute or whistle, with another hole at the natural placing of a thumb-hole on its other side. But the "flute" has become an object of contention, for sceptics claim that it is not a deliberately perforated bone but merely one that has been chewed by a large carnivore leaving its teeth marks behind. (There also seems to be just a slight prejudice within some academic circles against accepting that Neanderthals could have

< 131 >

possessed such a refined faculty as musical awareness.) Canadian musicologist Bob Fink has argued strenuously against such an interpretation, pointing out a number of factors – namely, that the spacing of the holes does not match that of the teeth of a likely culprit such as a wolf or hyena, certainly not a single bite at any rate; at least three of the holes are fairly well in line, which is also unlikely in a gnawed bone; the diameters of the holes are fairly even; the bone has responded to blowing by an accomplished flute-player by producing musical sounds, and most of the other bones found in the cave had been chewed at the ends. Also the bone was not split, which would have been the expected result of it being bitten in its central portion. Fink claims that the bone is musically sophisticated, and that the three notes are inescapably diatonic. But the hard truth is that there is no fully decisive evidence for or against the argument, so the bone flute has to remain in limbo as an unproven instrument.

Other finds from the Neanderthal – Middle Palaeolithic – era remain similarly contentious, such as a mammoth long bone unearthed in Belgium in 1976, which is engraved with twelve grooves, apparently intentionally carved by humans. It dates back about 45,000 years, and various explanations as to its function have been made. One has been that it was a sound-generating device, specifically a rasp or scraper that makes a noise when a stick or bone plectrum is dragged across its grooves – a bit like a skiffle board of modern times. Rasps have been found in numerous archaeological contexts worldwide, prompting anthropologist Richard Rudgley to remark that "Neanderthal people may have made at least simple musical instruments, and if they did so then the rasp would be among the more likely candidates".[124] He adds, though, that the evidence of a Middle Palaeolithic musical tradition is slim. But there are tantalizing clues. For example, archaeological excavation at the Middle Palaeolithic cave site called Prolom II, in the Crimea, yielded over 100 pierced animal bones that seem to be more like whistles than anything else – they certainly produce strong, shrill

< 132 >

sounds when blown. It has been suggested that these may not have been musical instruments as such, but rather used for decoy purposes in imitating bird or animal sounds. Even if this is true, they represent the conscious creation of sound-making devices, and would surely have soon led to musical instruments and the dawn of music. (It is now known from skeletal examination that Neanderthals would have been able to sing.)

When we come to the Upper Palaeolithic, the era of our modern ancestors, painted caves and the presumed use of lithophones, the evidence for conscious acoustic awareness becomes overwhelming. A haul of bone percussion instruments was discovered in a hut constructed out of mammoth bones at Mezin in the Ukraine. They included mammoth skull bones, hip bones, shoulder-blade and jaw bones, all decorated with ochre, and were accompanied by a "castanet bracelet" and two rattles made of ivory. This Stone Age "orchestra" is dated to *c.*18,000BC. The bone implements showed clear signs of use. In 1976 percussionists from the Kiev State Orchestra successfully used the pieces, and there was no doubt about their percussive effectiveness. Despite this, there are still scholars who doubt that they were used as musical instruments. This is also the attitude displayed by some towards a 24,000-year-old reindeer antler with a polished end, found in the Czech Republic, which other experts identify as a drumstick. It was found in association with a richly ornamented human burial, so it may well have been the percussive tool of a shaman.[125]

A number of presumably Palaeolithic bullroarers have also been found in some of the French caves. One from La Roche de Birol is a length of reindeer antler incised with geometric designs; when it is whirled around on a string it produces a remarkably loud roaring noise, thereby creating a profoundly eerie effect within the cave.

The best evidence for Upper Palaeolithic wind instruments is provided by delicately made bird, bear and reindeer hollow-bone pipes, dating to the millennia around 18,000BC, which have been

< 133 >

found in caves and other Palaeolithic sites from France to Russia. They have variously between three and seven holes in them, and some are decorated with chevrons, notches and other designs. They are generally interpreted as being cross-blown flutes or whistles.[126] Cambridge music archaeologist Graeme Lawson has closely examined some of these objects and asserts that the finger-holes are well defined, and that the pipes are capable of playing tuneful music rather than disorganized noise. Their "full-throated" output would have been amplified further by the acoustics of a cave.[127] These pipes are the oldest known musical instruments in Europe or Asia.

Bone whistles have also been found dating from the Neolithic era, examples include a bird bone with two finger-holes from Cougnac, a hollowed stag's antler pierced with three holes from a cave near Poitiers, a smoothed long bone with four equidistant holes unearthed in a Neolithic burial site in Germany, and a whistle made, somewhat disturbingly, from a human thigh bone found in the Neolithic occupation level of a cave in the former Yugoslavia.[128]

Musical instruments made from perishable, organic materials, such as wood, string or animal skins, would not, of course, have survived from the either the Palaeolithic or Neolithic eras, though there are a few clues as to their one-time existence. A depiction on the walls of Les Trois Frères cave shows two beasts near a man, dressed in a bison skin, who holds a bow-like object. The scene has been variously interpreted as a disguised archer creeping up on his prey, or as a shaman charming two animals with a musical bow. Reznikoff supported the latter view, pointing out that the musical bow is an excellent support to the voice and gives the possibility of varying pitch; he figured it may well have been used in the resonant rituals of the caves.[129]

As far as the Neolithic era goes, we know that drums were certainly in use in Europe from at least the fifth millennium BC, because among a number of miniature clay objects found at the site of Ovcarovo in Bulgaria were three cylindrical drums. "It seems likely that the model

< 134 >

Chinese Neolithic Flutes

Six complete, playable multi-note flutes have been excavated at the early Neolithic site of Jiahu in Henan Province, China, which radiocarbon dating suggests was occupied between 7000 and 5700BC. The complete flutes were found with the fragments of about thirty others in radiocarbon-dated excavation layers. These 9,000-year-old instruments are made from the bones of cranes and were exquisitely crafted. They have, variously, between five and eight holes, and must have been played in the vertical fashion.

One of the flutes, with seven holes, was free of cracks, and was therefore selected to be tested acoustically. The tone of the whole tube is G_5 or F_5. Its tonal scale is the ancestor of either the six-tone Qing Shan scale or the seven-tone Xia Shi scale, both of which were only documented 6,000 years later. A Chinese folk song was played on the flute by Taoying Xu, and this was recorded (it can be heard on the website of *Nature* magazine at http://www.nature.com). The flute produces a "breathy" sound, a little reminiscent of pan-pipes.

Source: Juzhong Zhang, Garman Harbottle, Changsui Wang and Zhaochen Kongs
"Oldest Playable Musical Instrument Found at Jiahu Early Neolithic site in China" in
Nature, no. 401, 23 September 1999, (366–368).

drums were replicas of full-scale drums that would have been beaten to accompany the religious ceremonies of this prehistoric community," Rudgley suggests.[130] Further, more than sixty Neolithic clay drums, ranging from large-scale bass drums to much smaller kinds, have been found in Germany alone, about half of them *in megalithic tombs*.

< 135 >

Modern replicas were made of some of these, and skins of uncured leather were stretched across their tops in the probable fashion of the originals (examples of Neolithic hourglass-shaped drums from Germany and Poland have decorative ceramic notches on their sides that would have been used as anchors for fixing and tightening the drum membrane). They played well.

* * *

The cumulative evidence leaves no room for any reasonable doubt that wind and percussion instruments, at least, (there may have been others) were in use in the Neolithic era, and quite possibly in the Upper Palaeolithic age – and perhaps even as far back as Neanderthal times (Middle Palaeolithic). Natural, sound-producing objects such as calcite formations in caves were also used to elicit acoustic effects from the Palaeolithic era onwards. The acoustic investigations of megalithic monuments and other prehistoric ritual places, as described in the previous two chapters, are therefore eminently justified. If anything, they are a belatedly welcome research development.

< 136 >

CHAPTER TEN

Old Sounds in the New World

As we are at last beginning to become aware of the ritual use of sound in prehistoric Europe and Asia, it is time to ask if similar evidence exists of ancient acoustic effects in the New World of the Americas. The experience of sound and music is, after all, universal and various strands of recent research have indicated that human beings are "wired" for musical sound. Experiments at Harvard University in the United States have shown that babies show a preference for consonant melodies when subjected to both consonant and dissonant sounds. Other research, using twins, has indicated that the ability to recognize pitch – telling whether a melody has correct notes and is not off-key – is hereditary. And work at Leicester University, England, has demonstrated that a child can remember a melody it hears while still in the womb. Sound, music and human sensibility go together.

In any case, it seems likely that American Indians originated in the Old World of Eurasia, and would have brought with them archaic knowledge and beliefs about sound when they moved across the lost land bridge of Beringia that once linked Siberia with Alaska.

KNOCK ON ROCK

Just as in Europe and Asia, ringing rocks in ancient America were venerated. These features are relatively rare, but about seven are known in the American Southwest and southern California. Most are associated with prehistoric rock-art. A good example still *in situ* occurs in the Menifee Valley of western Riverside County, California, about 120 kilometres (75 miles) southwest of downtown Los Angeles – its exact location is kept secret because of fears of vandalism. The valley was once part of the territory traditionally occupied by the Luiseño people. Catherine Saubel, a 70-year-old Indian, found herself "awe-struck" when she was taken to the valley's ringing rock. She had known about ringing rocks all her life, but until then had never actually seen or heard one.[131] Rock-art is found throughout the Menifee Valley and consists mainly of abstract signs carved into the scattered rocks and boulders, though a few weathered paintings in black and red also survive. The ringing rock is one of a group of boulders at the north end of a ridge. It is granite, about 1 metre (3 feet) across, and deep hollows or "cupules" have been worn into its surface by human effort. The rock rings clearly, like a chime, when lightly struck with a small stone.[132] When struck in different places with various sizes of stone a range of tones can be produced. The special sonorous properties of the rock are enhanced because it is balanced on a giant boulder, with considerable air space beneath.

Little is known about the usage of ringing rocks in ancient California, but what ethnography of the region exists links them with trail shrine functions and with girls' puberty ceremonies. Concerning the latter, ethnologist Constance DuBois wrote in 1908 that one of the elders would sing in accompaniment to the "ringing stones" while others danced.

Ken Hedges, curator at the San Diego Museum of Man, has identified other ringing rocks in the California region. The best known example is Bell Rock, now found in the courtyard of the Bowers Museum in Santa Ana but formerly located in the Santa Ana Mountains of Orange County. It weighs about 7 tons and is marked with numerous cupules. One historian said of the rock: "Around this granite boulder native Indians gathered in ancient times. With stone pestles they pounded upon it and the canyon rang with the clear tones of this primitive bell."[133] Another example exists at the site of Pahpahwits in Tulare

< 138 >

County; it is a much smaller boulder than Bell Rock, but is nevertheless marked with cupules. One ethnographic account states that at Pahpahwits it was the practice of passing Yokuts Indians to pause and "ring the bells" – meaning that they struck "thin ledges of rock extended from the ground", which issued bell-like sounds. Interestingly, this description does not sound like the known Pahpahwits ringing rock. A third Californian ringing rock is identified in museum records as existing – or having once existed – on the north bank of the San Dieguito River, in San Diego County. In the Southwest region, ringing rocks have been noted in conjunction with rock-art sites at Zion Wash, near Virginia City, Nevada, and at Cocoraque Butte in southern Arizona, a site associated with the now-vanished prehistoric Indian culture, the Hohokam.

Much further to the north, in North Dakota, there is a different type of acoustic boulder site known as the Writing Rock, found at the foot of a hill that has ancient burial mounds on its summit. The rock is situated at Fort Ransom in the Cheyenne River Valley, an area replete with petroglyphs and archaeological sites. The area as a whole is more than 480 kilometres (300 miles) northwest of Minneapolis. The boulder is of white granite, and carved with cupules (some of which are thought to be relatively recent), and four grooves each more than 1.5 metres (5 feet) long. Rock-art expert Jack Steinbring has proposed that making cupules and grooves involves "rhythmic sound and action" that can in itself be trance-inducing.[134] It is located close to a natural spring and has panoramic views, the kind of conditions that were considered ideal for vision-questing sites. Springs were also associated with the spirits that helped shamans "write" on rocks, and with rainmaking rituals. The rock's location has very special "amphitheatre acoustics": standing at Writing Rock it is possible to hear people talking from right across the valley and at other distant points. "The pounding of the boulder may have been heard all over the valley," University of Minnesota anthropologist Kevin Callahan further observes.

< 139 >

Steinbring has noted two rock-art sites in Saskatchewan, Canada, that may have made use of acoustical effects. Excavation at one of them, the Herschel Petroglyph Site, has revealed numerous bison bones remaining from offerings placed at the base of a monolithic rock that is covered with hundreds of pecked cupules. The site may also have been used as a "buffalo jump" – a place where herds of bison were stampeded over a precipice to be killed and butchered below. "The location is resonant and may amplify sounds at times," Steinbring reports.[135] He suspects that the sounds of making the cupules in the site's acoustic space would have mimicked thundering herds of bison. A similar situation might have prevailed at the other location, known as Swift Current, where a richly decorated rock has the image of a bison pecked into it. These observations of course parallel Waller's ideas about the ritual use of acoustics to mimic the sound of hoofed animals depicted in the French cave paintings (see Chapter 8).

Travelling southwards in the Americas, similar traditions can be detected. For example, the ancient Maya of southern Mexico and adjacent regions also had a penchant for knocking on natural objects – stalactites, to be precise. Stalactites were sacred to them, and water that dripped from them was so holy that even deep within cave systems they would place special stone troughs to catch the precious fluid, which they referred to as "virgin water". Some stalactites and other calcite formations that might coincidentally suggest the shape of a human or animal figure were sometimes subtly enhanced by human intervention – a similar practice to that found in some ancient European caves, such as those in Minoan Crete, where modifications were made to and offerings wedged among the folds of stalactites.[136] It is not surprising, then, that, when struck, two mighty stalactites in the ancient Mayan ritual cave of Lol-Tun in the Yucatán Peninsula have been found to issue a deeply resonant sound that rolls through the surrounding cavernous space (see Plate 32). The Maya too, it seems, had lithophones.

< 140 >

In the famous Late Classic (*c.*AD600–830) Mayan-Toltec ceremonial complex of Chichén Itzá, Yucatán, there are groups of phallic-shaped stones (see Plate 33). It has been widely claimed that when these are hit they issue ringing sounds, but this may be true of only selected phallus stones in the complex, or ones that have been destroyed, because none of the phalluses in the one group tested during our visit produced any noteworthy acoustic effects. It is said that in the 1920s, the field team with one of the fathers of Mayan archaeology, Sylvanus Morley, laid out some of these stone phalluses in rows like a xylophone, and played Christmas carols on them! There are doubtless many more ritual ringing rocks throughout the Americas, but a full, scholarly census has yet to be compiled.

TALKING TEMPLES

In the ancient Americas acoustic consciousness took other forms as well – notably in its presence at oracle temples. Probably the most famous example in this regard is the impressive Mayan ceremonial complex of Palenque, surrounded by hills and jungle in northern Chiapas, Mexico. Palenque reached its golden age in the seventh century AD under the rule of Lord Pacal, whose remarkable tomb was found beneath the Temple of the Inscriptions. What has captured public attention, though, is the acoustics of a group of temples on the eastern side of the complex: the so-called "Cross group", consisting of the temples of the Cross, the Foliated Cross, and the Sun. These pyramid-platform temples stand around an elevated plaza about 200 metres (nearly 660 feet) across, and it has been noticed that people standing at the top of each of these can, against all logic, communicate in a perfectly normal talking voice with one another, the sound carrying despite the distances involved. One anecdote refers to the "altered" acoustic quality of the space between the temples. Mayan guides at Palenque can communicate with one another across the entire complex with low whistles because of the unusual acoustics that seem to be present at the place. There are also contentious claims that some of the

< 141 >

passages and stone channels beneath and within some of the structures at Palenque could have acted as voice tubes or channels for acoustic effects perpetrated by the priests. As another father of Mayan archaeology, Eric Thompson, remarked regarding the underground passages, they "might have been used for a little religious hocus-pocus".[137]

A temple in the Postclassic period (c.AD1000–AD1540) Mayan complex of Tulúm, on the Yucatán coast, is said to give a clear, long-range whistle or howl when the velocity and direction of the wind is correct. Mayan site guides claim that it is a warning of incoming hurricanes and big storms from the Caribbean. (Perhaps the acoustic effect created by the wind flow in the temple architecture was considered to be the voice of a storm god – one of the temples in the complex, and possibly the one implicated in the described effect, is dedicated to the "Descending God".)

A film crew working on a Mayan pyramid at Tikal, Guatemala, noticed that a stone feature there produced a "clear, short sustained sound" when tapped. It then found that much of the pyramid was constructed from the same kind of stone. When anyone walked down from the top of the pyramid platform, the impact of their feet on the stone steps produced gong-like sounds. It is perhaps not a coincidence that the name "Tikal" means "Place Where Spirit Voices Are Heard". There are other accounts of Mayan temple acoustic effects, but currently most remain anecdotal and are controversial (see also below).

More certain evidence of ancient acoustical sophistication has been found in the Andes region of South America. One example is the temple of Chavín de Huantar, located at the confluence of two rivers in northern Peru, which was a very important shamanic cult centre at the heart of prehistoric oracle and pilgrimage traditions. The cult was active from c.900 to c.200BC, and its influence spread over vast distances. One aspect of ritual activities conducted there involved the use of the hallucinogenic San Pedro cactus, which is depicted on a bas-relief at the site. The first structure at the site is known now as the Old Temple, and later another

< 142 >

wing, the "New Temple", was added. The Old Temple is a windowless building and deep inside its structure is a cruciform chamber containing a monolith 4.5 metres (nearly 15 feet) tall called the Lanzón, which has been carved to represent a fearsome, snarling deity. A curious gallery above this chamber is thought to have allowed hidden priests to give oracular voice to the Lanzón deity.[138] Also hidden away inside the Old Temple is a labyrinth of mysterious passageways that were connected by stairways, vents and drainage canals. There are more than 500 metres (1,650 feet) of these vents and drainage channels, far exceeding any simple engineering requirements. It is thought that they formed an awesomely impressive sound system. It seems the temple may have roared with a thunderous sound caused by water passing through the channels. An archaeologist conducted an experiment at the site in which he poured water into the drainage channels and amplified the sound of the rushing water by closing and opening vents. The temple reverberated with a sound that the archaeologist compared to applause.[139]

Something similar seems to have been created at the equally ancient but far distant pilgrimage centre of Tiahuanaco, in the high Andes of western Bolivia, close to Lake Titicaca. The centrepiece of this ceremonial city is a pyramid 17 metres (nearly 56 feet) tall, known as the Akapana. This is, in effect, a model mountain: it contains materials brought in from the sacred peaks of the surrounding area, and like Chavín it was over-engineered with water channels. During stormy weather it would have allowed water from the sunken court on its summit to flow down its external terraces while at the same time passing through an elaborate internal drainage system. Large drains in the system would have created a rumbling acoustic effect like the sound of the thunder in the mountains.[140]

In both these examples, the deep roaring sound would presumably have been interpreted as the voice of the thunder or rain god, and probably used as an acoustic matrix, a kind of audio inkblot test, out of which oracular pronouncements could be deciphered.

< 143 >

ECHOES OF ANCIENT AMERICA

Effects produced by reflected sound have been found at sacred places in the Americas just as they have in the Old World. Steven Waller has been active in searching out such places, using the same techniques as he did in the French caves. To date, he has identified dozens of rock-art sites in the Americas that have distinctive echo properties. For example, after analysing acoustic data he collected in Horseshoe Canyon, Utah, he found that the five art sites there exactly match the five locations within the canyon that possess the greatest intensity of echoing. Other acoustical rock-art sites are to be found in well-known pre-Columbian Indian sacred areas, such as Chaco Canyon and Bandelier National Monument (both in New Mexico), Wupatki Anasazi complex and Painted Rocks State Park (both in Arizona), and in the Hueco Tanks rock-art area of Texas, as well as a great many more lesser known locations.[141] He found the same kind of effects in a Chumash Indian painted cave near Santa Barbara, California, as he had found in the French Palaeolithic caves. Waller is convinced that echoes were a key feature in the siting of rock-art for many ancient peoples around the world.

Echoes occur in other pre-Columbian American contexts. Teotihuacán was a vast ceremonial city covering 25 square kilometres (nearly 10 square miles), founded by an unknown culture almost 2,000 years ago. It had its heyday between AD350 and 650, and its extensive ruins still exist to the northeast of modern-day Mexico City. The ruins consist of great axial roads, a ritual cave (modified by humans, it has resonant qualities amplifying the human voice), pyramids, plazas, living quarters, workshops and many temples. One of the more important of the temples is dedicated to the Feathered Serpent – known later on to the Maya as Kukulcan and to the Aztecs as Quetzalcóatl. A percussive noise such as a hand clap (which provides an intense burst of wide-spectrum sound energy) made within the temple compound at a precise spot between a small satellite shrine on the axis of the main temple and the entrance platform of the temple

< 144 >

itself produces a sharp, distinctive echo from the temple that ends in a descending-pitch "chirp" reminiscent of a bird call. Anywhere else in the compound and the sound of a hand clap is ineffectual, its sound becoming lost without an echo.

This is a curiosity, but it becomes more interesting when the stepped pyramid known as El Castillo at the Chichén Itzá complex is considered (see Plate 34). This ceremonial city was in use among the Maya between *c.*AD600 and 830, and thereafter was influenced by the Toltecs from the north for several centuries longer. El Castillo is a tiered platform, which has a temple on its summit dedicated to Kukulcan. At the equinoxes (21 March and 21 September) there is a fabulous display of visual symbolism here: as the sun sets, a serrated shadow created by one of the stepped edges of the pyramid platform is thrown onto the balustrade of one of the staircases leading up to the summit temple. This shadow appears to move as the sun moves, and the appearance is given of a diamond-back serpent (the diamond-back rattlesnake is common to the area) slithering out of its temple and down the platform stairway. This impression is enhanced as the shadow connects up with the stone carving of a serpent's head at the bottom of the balustrade. This display is now quite famous, but what is less well known is that there seems to be a soundtrack to this symbolism. A percussive sound – again a handclap provides a suitable test sound source – made at a precise spot between the north face of El Castillo and the satellite shrine known as the Temple of Venus produces a sharp echo, with a descending-pitch, bird-like chirp sound (see Plate 35).

Californian acoustics expert David Lubman has made a special study of the El Castillo effect. "The physics of the chirped echo can be explained quite simply as periodic reflections from step faces," he says. Then adds, cuttingly: "But until now, no one has bothered to do so."[142] Basically, the curious echo is caused by what is known as the "picket fence effect", in which soundwaves are reflected off a close

< 145 >

sequence of similar-dimension surfaces – in El Castillo's case it is the stone steps of the staircase – and the sequential or periodic reflected sound is perceived as a "tonal echo". The origin of the chirp at the end of this tonal echo is summarized by Lubman in the no-frills terms common to technicians:

" Elementary geometrical analysis shows that the path length for reflections arriving from higher steps increases slightly and gradually. The longer path length translates into a lengthening echo periodicity. This imparts a noticeable downward glide to the pitch of the tonal echo. This gives rise to a chirped echo. Chirped echoes are known to acousticians. "[143]

But Lubman goes on to make a further, acute observation that is anything but dry and technical. He noted that the chirped echo is remarkably similar to the primary call of the Quetzal bird, an exotic, brightly coloured bird that is now an endangered species but was once the great spirit bird of the ancient Maya. The Mayan culture was a rainforest one, and it has been demonstrated (see Chapter 2) that sound and hearing is primary to such people because of the close, dense nature of their environment, and that bird calls can be associated with the sounds of spirits. It is known that the Maya used the colourful plumage of the Quetzal bird for their ceremonial headdresses, and it was doubtless associated with the Feathered Serpent. Lubman has closely analysed the primary call of the (free, non-captive) Quetzal bird with El Castillo's chirped echo, and while the sounds are not identical he has found them to be extremely similar.[144] He envisages the priests and priestesses of Chichén Itzá standing at the appropriate place making percussive sounds to accompany the visual display of the descending serpent. Sound, it has been suggested, was a spiritual thing, a mystery, to pre-modern people, and such a *son et lumière* experience would have been vivid and awesome for onlookers then in a way we can never appreciate today. To them, Kukulcan would have been made manifest.

< 146 >

There is an additional fact: the Quetzal bird's primary call attracts other members of the species: did the great ritual shadow play and soundtrack at El Castillo actually call the sacred bird in from the surrounding jungle?

Despite the reasonable nature of Lubman's general suggestion, it remains something of a contentious issue for some archaeologists of the Maya, although others are more open to it. El Castillo, although to some extent restored, is much as it would have been in its prime, so there is no question of its acoustic effect being substantially different from what is heard today.

A further observation can be added, for the present author discovered a similar chirped echo at the so-called palace building at Sayil in Yucatán. As usual, it could be elicited only from a particular spot, and that place was adjacent to where one of the mysterious ceremonial, dead-straight causeways associated with the ancient Maya enters the plaza that contains the palace. This exactly corresponds to where the sound has to be produced to elicit El Castillo's chirped echo. At Chichén Itzá the causeway (*sacbe*) from the Sacred Cenote (sinkhole) enters the Great Plaza containing El Castillo at the Temple of Venus. Were ritual sounds associated with these mysterious ceremonial roads? There are more questions than answers.

The El Castillo effect may indeed be a genuine acoustic fossil, and a sceptical attitude, which is held towards it by some conservative scholars, may be more valid in the case of the other well-known echo effect at Chichén Itzá – the odd acoustics present at the Great Ballcourt. The ballgame in Mayan culture was both a sport and a ritual. It is thought that the losers were decapitated, and, according to the Mayan sacred text the *Popol Vuh*, ballcourts represented the entrance to the underworld. There are many anecdotes confirming that a whisper in the temple at one end of the Chichén Itzá court can be heard 168 metres (550 feet) away in the temple at the other end (though the author was unable to replicate this effect). There has been criticism, though, that

< 147 >

the existing temple ruins do not represent the forms of the original temples; in addition, the way they have crumbled has created curved masonry structures, which would be likely to reflect sound and create a "whispering gallery" effect. So the acoustic anomaly at Chichén Itzá's Great Ballcourt may be an accidental consequence of the passage of the centuries rather than a genuine acoustic survival from the Mayan past. In acoustic archaeology, not all sounds are equal.

* * *

Overall, there is adequate evidence to suggest that pre-Columbian Native Americans did pay attention to unusual acoustic effects, and used them to express or augment their beliefs and cosmology by means of various forms of acoustic symbolism, just as did the ancient cultures living half a world away and thousands of years earlier. It remains unclear, though, exactly how far this manipulation of acoustic effects was consciously carried out, and it awaits more thoroughgoing research.

< 148 >

EPILOGUE

Clap Your Hands!

Like much of archaeology dealing with prehistory, acoustic archaeology is largely a matter of interpretation. Ways have to be found of deriving evidence, and then that has to be evaluated in the context of what else is known. Acoustic archaeology is embryonic, and it has a lot of growing to do, but already important lines of inquiry are presenting themselves, and some telling evidence is emerging. The work in Europe and Asia exploring the Palaeolithic and Neolithic use of stalactites and musical instruments shows clearly that human beings had an awareness of sound from the earliest times, and that it is likely that they regarded it as a manifestation of the supernatural in one form or another. The research in which modern sound equipment is used to explore the resonance and echo effects in caves and megalithic monuments produces results that are less certain and more genuinely interpretative, yet its findings are suggestive and promise fresh ways of gaining insight into the use of monuments that have for so long remained enigmatic. Indeed, in the light of the long prehistory of human interaction with sound, it becomes unreasonably conservative to doubt that there would be important acoustic aspects to megalithic monuments, or that the dramatic resonance of caves would have been ignored by Stone Age people.

The acoustic aspects must not be overstated, however. Sound must not be turned into an explain-all of prehistoric sacred sites. We can tell that Palaeolithic rock-art, for example, was about other things than the echoing characteristics of certain cave walls: we can see how visual elements were important, too, such as the bump in a rock-surface that became the shoulder-blade of a painted animal, or the curve of an overhang or rock projection that provided part of the outline of a painted creature's back, belly or head. In Chapter 1 it was shown that shadows, too, probably played an elusive role. So visual elements were of great significance and indicate that Stone Age people had a rather "dreamy" way of looking at things. The probable acoustic aspects are best seen simply as other factors that came into play. Whether visual or auditory, the underlying sense seems to have been that rock surfaces were regarded as the interface between the physical and spiritual worlds – that spirits could emerge from rock faces and fissures just as entranced shamans could pass through the rock surface into the spirit otherworld. It is also important to remember that during rituals both the visual and auditory aspects of a site would have been greatly enhanced to those in altered states of mind and would have taken on completely different levels of significance. So we not only have to battle against the gulf of time between ourselves and the megalith builders and cave artists, we also have to overcome the fact that we are not experiencing their sacred places in the same mental states as they did.

So it is not that the acoustic effects found at prehistoric sites are of some special, overriding importance, but rather that such aspects have been ignored for too long. *Acoustic archaeology is about the healing of our research "deafness"*; it is giving us an extra sense to use in our investigation of ancient sacred places.

Books on prehistoric monuments, ancient temples or rock-art rarely have any mention of acoustic factors in their indexes – that, I hope, will change over the coming years – but it will only come about by a change of attitude. As Steven Waller has urged, we should no longer be content to face a panel of rock-art, or enter a megalithic space, and simply stare around mutely. As well as using our eyes, we must start using our ears as a matter of course when at an ancient sacred place. As circumstances allow, we should clap our hands, shout, hum, whistle, sing. And then listen. Who knows but that the spirits of the place might speak to us, and tell us things that we might otherwise miss?

< 150 >

Clap Your Hands!

With the now ongoing restoration of Stone Age "soundtracks" come new concerns about conservation. It is, of course, important to preserve the physical fabric of a monument (and that is often difficult enough to guarantee), but the less tangible aspects need guarding as well. There is an argument in many cases to try to preserve the visibility of a site and the view from it, for these visual factors often seem to have been key concerns for those who originally set up a site. Now, additionally, we should try to preserve the acoustic environment of a monumental site, for this can be all too readily damaged or destroyed by the thoughtless erection of walls and fences around it, the building of modern structures or embankments near it, or the placing of any other impediment to what would have been the original passage of soundwaves through and around a site. If we are now learning how to recover the "soundtracks" of remote antiquity, it would be a pity not to have a chance to play them again.

References & Notes

Dates after book titles indicate date of first publication.
Numbers in (parentheses) at end of an entry indicate page numbers.

PART ONE

1. Jaynes, J., *The Origin of Consciousness in the Breakdown of the Bicameral Mind*, Houghton Mifflin, Boston, 1976.
2. Levy-Bruhl, Lucien, *Primitive Mythology*, (1935), University of Queensland Press, St. Lucia, 1983.
3. Theodoratus, Dorothy, and LaPena, Frank, "Wintu Sacred Geography of Northern California", *Sacred Sites, Sacred Places*, Carmichael, D., Hubert, J., Reeves, B., and Schanche, A., (eds.), Routledge, London, 1994, (20–31).
4. Lewis-Williams, J. David, and Dowson, T., "Through the Veil: San Rock Paintings and the Rock Face", *South African Archaeological Bulletin* 45, 1990, (5–16).
5. Lewis-Williams, J. David, and Clottes, Jean, "The Mind in the Cave – the Cave in the Mind: Altered Consciousness in the Upper Palaeolithic", *Anthropology of Consciousness*, vol. 9, no.1, 1998, (13–21).
6. Siegel, R.K., and Jarvik, M.E., "Drug-induced Hallucinations in Animals and Man", *Hallucinations*, Siegel, R.K. and West, L.J., (eds.), John Wiley, New York, 1975, (81–162).
7. Whitley, David, *A Guide to Rock Art Sites in Southern California and Southern Nevada*, Mountain Press, Missoula, 1996.
8. Rajnovich, Grace, *Reading Rock Art – Interpreting the Indian Rock Paintings of the Canadian Shield*, Natural Heritage/ Natural History Inc., Toronto, 1994.
9. Carpenter, E., and McLuhan, M., "Acoustic Space", *Explorations in Communication*, (1960), Carpenter, E., and McLuhan, M., (eds.), Jonathan Cape, London, 1970, (65–70).
10. Carpenter, E., *Eskimo Realities*, Holt, Rinehart and Winston, New York, 1973.
11. Carpenter and McLuhan, 1960/1970, *op. cit.*
12. Gell, A., "The Language of the Forest: Landscape and Phonological Iconism in Umeda", *The Anthropology of Landscape*, Hirsch, E., and O'Hanlon, M., (eds.), Oxford University Press, Oxford, 1995, (232–254).
13. See also (and particularly) Feld, S., "Waterfalls of Song: An Acoustemology of Place Resounding in Bosavi, Papua New Guinea", *Senses of Place*, Feld, S., and Basso, K., (eds.), School of American Research Press, Santa Fe, 1996, (91–135).
14. La Barre, W., *The Ghost Dance*, Delta, New York, 1972.
15. Jackson, A., "Sound and Ritual", *Man* 3, no.2, 1968, (293–299).
16. Tuzin, D., "Miraculous Voices: The Auditory Experience of Numinous Objects", *Current Anthropology*, vol. 25, no.5, 1984, (579–596).
17. Luck, G. *Arcana Mundi*, (1985), Crucible, 1987.

18. ibid.
19. Katz, F., and Dobkin De Rios, M., "Whistling in Peruvian Ayahuasca Healing Sessions", *Journal of American Folklore*, vol. 84, no. 333, 1971, (320–327).
20. Shah, Tahir, *Trail of Feathers*, Weidenfeld and Nicolson, London, 2001.
21. Wasson, G., "The Hallucinogenic Fungi of Mexico", (1961), *The Psychedelic Reader*, Weil, G., Metzner, R., and Leary, T., (eds.), University Books, New York, 1965, (23–38).
22. Dobkin De Rios, M., and Katz, F., "Some Relationships between Music and Hallucinogenic Ritual: The 'Jungle Gym' in Consciousness", *Ethos*, vol. 3, no. 1, 1975, (64–76).
23. ibid.
24. Olsen, D., "Music–Induced Altered State of Consciousness among Warao Shamans", *Journal of Latin American Lore*, vol.1, no.1, 1975, (19–33).
25. La Barre, W., "Anthropological Perspectives on Hallucinations and Hallucinogens", *Hallucinations*, Siegel, R.K., and West, L.J., (eds.), 1975, *op. cit.* (9–52).
26. Tuzin, D., 1984, *op. cit.*
27. ibid.
28. ibid.
29. Needham, R., "Percussion and Transition", *Man* 2, 1967, (606–614).
30. Huxley, F., "Anthropology and ESP", *Science and ESP*, Smythies, J., (ed.), Routledge and Kegan Paul, London, 1967. Cited in Needham, R., 1967, *op. cit.*
31. Neher, A., "A Physiological Explanation of Unusual Behaviour in Ceremonies Involving Drums", *Human Biology*, vol.34, 1962, (151–160).
32. Jilek, W., *Salish Indian Mental Health and Culture Change: Psychohygienic and Therapeutic Aspects of the Guardian Spirit Ceremonial*, Holt, Rinehart and Winston, New York, 1974. Cited in Harner, M., *The Way of the Shaman*, (1980), HarperSanFrancisco, 1990.
33. Goodman, F., *Where the Spirits Ride the Wind*, Indiana University Press, Bloomington, 1990.
34. Neher, A., 1962, *op. cit.*
35. Maxfield, M., *Effects of Rhythmic Drumming on EEG and Subjective Experiences*, Ph.D. dissertation, Institute of Transpersonal Psychology, Menlo Park, 1990. Cited by Woodside, L., Kumar, V. and Pekala, R., "Monotonous Percussion Drumming and Trance Postures: A Controlled Evaluation of Phenomenological Effects", *Anthropology of Consciousness*, vol. 8, no. 2–3, 1997, (69–87).
36. Tempest, W., *Infrasound and Low Frequency Vibration*, Academic Press, London, 1976.
37. Actual frequency limits are usually around 16 Hz for the normal adult, and 14 Hz for a child.
38. Non-acousticians often get confused about the role of decibels in sound measurement. A *decibel* (dB), one tenth of a bel, describes noise level relative to the threshold of human hearing. In other words, it is the common measure of sound pressure. A *phon* is a unit of perceived loudness. Loudness in phons is given by the number of decibels above an agreed reference level (if you want to know what that is: 20 µ Pa – of a pure 1 kHz frequency sound, which is judged by listeners to be of equal loudness with the original). A sound has the intensity of 100 phons if it is 100 decibels lower than the softest sound of that pitch audible to the human ear.
39. Broner, N., "The Effects of Low Frequency Noise on People - A Review", *Journal of Sound and Vibration*, vol. 58, no. 4, 1978, (483–500).
40. Tempest, W. 1976, *op. cit.*
41. ibid.
42. ibid.
43. ibid.
44. Broner, N., 1978, *op. cit.*

< 153 >

45. Tandy, V., "Something in the Cellar", *Journal of the Society for Psychical Research*, vol. 64.3, no. 860, 2000, (129–140).
46. Swanson, David, "Non-Lethal Acoustic Weapons: Facts, Fiction, and the Future" http://www.unh.edu/orps/nonlethality/pub/presentations/1999/swanson/swanson.html. Cited in Tandy, *ibid.*
47. A standing wave occurs when identical waves travelling in opposite directions superimpose one on the other, creating the appearance of a stationary wave in which the nodes and antinodes (points of zero and maximum amplitude, troughs and crests) seem not to move. In the situation concerned here, the soundwaves of a standing wave within a cavity (the megalithic chamber in this case) travel out from the sound source to the walls (where there is an antinode) and reflect back.
48. Jaynes, J., 1976, *op. cit.*
49. Booth, M., *The Experience of Songs*, Yale University Press, New Haven, 1981. Cited in Tuzin, D., 1984, *op. cit.*
50. La Barre, W., 1975, *op. cit.*
51. Critchley, M., "Ecstatic and Synaesthetic Experiences during Musical Perception", *Music and the Brain*, Critchley, M., and Henson, R., (eds.), Heinemann Medical Books, London, 1977, (217–232).
52. F. Bowers, 1969. Cited in Critchley, M., 1977, *op. cit.*
53. Critchley, M., 1977, *op. cit.*
54. *ibid.*
55. Merriam, A., *The Anthropology of Music*, Northwestern University Press, 1964.
56. Mayer-Gross and Stein, 1926. Cited in Critchley, M., 1977, *op. cit.*
57. Merriam, A., 1964, *op. cit.*
58. *Ibid.*
59. Scott, D., "Musicogenic Epilepsy (2)", in Critchley and Henson, (eds.), 1977, *op. cit.*, (354–364).
60. *ibid.*
61. *ibid.*
62. *ibid.*
63. Eliade, M., *Shamanism – Archaic Techniques of Ecstasy*, (1951), Princeton University Press, Princeton, 1964. Also see La Barre, W., 1975, *op. cit.*
64. Schoen, M., *The Effects of Music*, Kegan Paul, Trench, Trubner, London, 1927.
65. Critchley, M., "Musicogenic Epilepsy (1)", in Critchley and Henson, (eds.), 1977, *op. cit.*, (344–353).
66. Harrer, G., and Harrer, H., "Music, Emotion and Autonomic Function", in Critchley and Henson, (eds.), 1977, *op. cit.*, (202–216).
67. *ibid.*
68. Khan, Hazrat Inayat, *The Mysticism of Sound and Music*, (1991), Shambhala, Boston, 1996.
69. *ibid.*
70. West, J.A., *The Traveler's Key to Ancient Egypt*, Alfred A. Knopf, New York, 1985.
71. *ibid.*
72. Rowland, I., and Howe, Thomas Noble, (eds.), *Vitruvius: Ten Books on Architecture*, Cambridge University Press, Cambridge, 1999.
73. Lawson, G., Scarre, C., Cross, I., and Hills, C., "Mounds, megaliths, music and mind: some thoughts on the acoustical properties and purposes of archaeological spaces", *ARC*, vol. 15, no. 1, 1998, (111–134).
74. *ibid.*

PART TWO

75. The full technical description of the whole field study can be found in: Jahn, R.G., Devereux, P., and Ibison, M, "Acoustical resonances of assorted ancient structures", *Journal of the Acoustical Society of America*, vol. 99, no. 2, 1996, (649–658).
76. Cooke, Ian, *Mother and Sun – The Cornish Fogou*, Men-an-Tol Studio, Penzance, 1993.
77. Brennan, Martin, *The Stars and the Stones*, Thames and Hudson, London, 1983.

< 154 >

Reference & Notes

78. In theory, it is possible to calculate resonance frequencies from the known dimensions of monuments without actually visiting them. But in reality the major physical irregularities present at the actual sites tend to doom this approach. Nothing betters actual on-site acoustic surveys.

79. Riordain, S., *Antiquities of the Irish Countryside*, (1942), Routledge, London, 1991 (revised by De Valera, R.).

80. Barfield, L., and Hodder, M., "Burnt Mounds as Saunas, and the Prehistory of Bathing", *Antiquity*, no. 61, 1987.

81. Burton, P., "Mystery of the Burnt Mounds", *The Ley Hunter*, no. 117, 1992, (23–25).

82. O'Kelly, M.J., *Newgrange*, Thames and Hudson, London, 1982.

83. Lynch, F., "The use of the passage in certain passage graves as a means of communication rather than access", (1969), *Megaliths, Graves, and Ritual: Papers of the 3rd Atlantic Colloquium*, Daniel, G., and Kjaerum, P., (eds.), Jutland Archaeological Society Publication X1, 1973.

84. Devereux, P., and Jahn, R.G., "Preliminary investigations and cognitive considerations of the acoustical resonances of selected archaeological sites", *Antiquity*, vol. 70, no. 269, 1996, (665–666).

85. Watson, W., and Keating, D., "Architecture and sound: an acoustic analysis of megalithic monuments in prehistoric Britain", *Antiquity*, vol. 73, no. 280, 1999, (325–336).

86. *ibid.*

87. *ibid.*

88. Watson, A., "Listening to the Stones", paper delivered at the T.A.G. conference, 1996.

89. *ibid.*

90. Lynch, F., 1969/1973, *op. cit.*

91. Watson, W., and Keating, D., "The Architecture of Sound in Neolithic Orkney", *Neolithic Orkney in its European Context*, Ritchie, A., (ed.), McDonald Institute Monographs, Cambridge, 2000, (259–263). (Citing Henshall, A., "The Chambered Cairns", in *The Prehistory of Orkney*, Renfrew, C., (ed.), Edinburgh University Press, Edinburgh, 1985.)

92. Watson, W., and Keating, D., 2000, *op. cit.*

93. As quoted in Urqhuart, F., "Echoes of the past stand revealed at Stone Age sites", *The Scotsman*, 18 November 1999.

94. As quoted in Branagan, C., "Scientists sound out stone theory", *Reading Evening Post*, 28 October 1998.

95. Burl, A., "Coves: Structural Enigmas of the Neolithic", *Wiltshire Archaeological and Natural History Magazine*, vol. 82, 1988, (1–18).

96. Reznikoff, I., "On the Sound Dimension of Prehistoric Painted Caves and Rocks", undated typescript, and also a similar version with the same title in *Musical Signification*, Taratsi, E., (ed.), Mouton de Gruyter, Berlin, 1995, (541–557).

97. Reznikoff, I., and Dauvois, M., "La dimension sonore des grottes ornées", *Bulletin de la Soc. Préhist. Francaise*, vol. 85, no. 8, 1988, (238–246). See also Scarre, Chris, "Painting by Resonance", *Nature*, vol. 338, 30 March 1989, (382).

98. Reznikoff, I., undated/1995, *op. cit.*

99. *ibid.*

100. *ibid.*

101. Dauvois, M., "Son et musique paléolithiques", *Les Dossiers d'Archéologie*, no. 142, 1989. Cited in Lawson, G., *et al.*, 1998, *op. cit.*

102. Waller, S., "Sound reflection as an explanation for the content and context of rock art", *Rock Art Research*, vol. 10, no. 2, 1993, (91–101).

103. *ibid.*

104. Dayton, L., "Rock art evokes beastly echoes of the past", *New Scientist*, 28 November 1992, (14).

105. Waller, S., 1993, *op. cit.*

< 155 >

106. *ibid.*
107. *ibid.*
108. Dayton, L., 1992, *op. cit.*
109. Waller, I., 1993, *op. cit.*
110. Reznikoff, undated/1995, *op. cit.*
111. This is discussed in some depth in Bradley, R., *An Archaeology of Natural Places*, Routledge. London, 2000; also in Devereux, P., *The Sacred Place*, Cassell, London, 2000.
112. Fagg, B., "Rock Gongs and Slides", *Man* 57, no. 32, 1957, (30–32).
113. Dewi Bowen, personal communication, citing the research of local folk museum curator, the late John Richards.
114. Fagg, B., 1957, *op. cit.*
115. Vaughan, J., "Rock paintings and rock gongs among the Marghi of Nigeria", *Man* 62, no. 83, 1962. Cited in Merriam, A., 1964, *op. cit.*
116. Seidenfaden, E., "Rock Gongs and Rock Slides", *Man* 57, no. 32, 1957, (32).
117. Lauhakangas, R., "A Lithophonic Drum in Lake Onega", *Adoranten*, Scandinavian Society for Prehistoric Art, 1999, (42–43).
118. Fagg, B., 1957, *op. cit.*
119. Dams, L., "Preliminary findings at the 'Organ' sanctuary in the cave of Nerja, Malaga, Spain", *Oxford Journal of Archaeology*, vol. 3, no. 1, 1984, (1–13).
120. Dams, L., "Palaeolithic lithophones: descriptions and comparisons", *Oxford Journal of Archaeology*, vol. 4, no.1, 1985. (31–46)
121. *ibid.*
122. This was the case, at least, at the time Dams was doing her work in the 1980s.
123. Lawson, G., *et al.*, 1998, *op. cit.*
124. Rudgley, R., *Lost Civilisations of the Stone Age*, Century, London, 1998.
125. Palmer, D., and Pettitt, P., "In Search of Our Musical Roots", *Focus*, no. 105, August, 2001, (80–84).
126. Rudgley, R., 1998, *op. cit.*
127. Palmer, D., *et al.*, 2001, *op. cit.*
128. Megaw, J.V.S., "Penny Whistles and Prehistory", *Antiquity* XXXIV, 1960, (6–13).
129. Reznikoff, I., undated/1995, *op. cit.*
130. Rudgley, R., 1998, *op. cit.*
131. Hillinger, C., "Ancient Granite Rock Chimes Like a Bell", *San Francisco Chronicle*, 15 May 1991.
132. Hedges, K., "Petroglyphs in Menifee Valley", *Rock Art Papers*, no. 7, 1990, (75–82).
133. Cited in *ibid.*
134. Steinbring, J., "Comments", in Waller, S., 1993, *op. cit.*
135. *ibid.*
136. Bradley, R., 2000, *op. cit.*; Devereux, P., 2000, *op. cit.*
137. Thompson, J.E.S., *The Rise and Fall of Maya Civilisation*, (1954), University of Oklahoma Press, Norman, 1966.
138. Stone, Rebecca, *Art of the Andes: From Chavín to Inca*, Thames and Hudson, London, 1995.
139. Von Hagan, A., and Morris, C., *The Cities of the Andes*, Thames and Hudson, London, 1998.
140. Kolata, A., *Valley of the Spirits*, John Wiley, New York, 1996.
141. Waller gives a much longer list of echo sites in America on his website. Simply set your search engine to find "Steven Waller".
142. Lubman, D., "An archaeological study of chirped echo from the Mayan pyramid of Kukulkan at Chichén Itzá", paper given at a conference at the Acoustical Society of America, 12–16 October 1998.
143. Lubman in e-mail correspondence to Wayne Van Kirk on the Mayan Acoustics internet list, 1998.
144. The sounds can be heard and compared directly on the internet: see David Lubman's home page, accessible through the website of the Acoustical Society of America, Orange County Regional Chapter.

< 156 >

Index

(Numbers in *italics* refer to illustrations in the text)

< 158 >

$\mathcal{I}$ n $\mathcal{d}$ $\mathcal{e}$ x

< 159 >

24, 30
bird call imitations 28
healing rituals 32–3, 36,
  39–40
knowledge of drugs 37, 38,
  39, 59
out-of-body experiences 21,
  36, 41
Peruvian cult centre 142–3
spirit-helper 40
"writing" on rocks 139
singing 37, 39–41
  see also poetry
slit-gongs 42–3
"songwords, secret/sacred" 28
sound 29ff., 58–9
  amplifying 42, 43, 45, 70,
    123, 142, 143
  and the body 46–7, 50, 51,
    60–1
  focusing 104
  hallucinatory 60
  patterns/shape of 58, 69,
    89–90
    seeing 91–2
  reflected see echoes
  silent 43–5, 100
  supernatural 27–8
  see also acoustics; auditory/oral
    traditions; infrasound;
    synaesthesia
"sounding vessels" 18, 68–9, 69
souterrains 81
speech:
  acoustical experimentation 98
  imitating 42
  and intersensory perception
    58
"spirit holes" 94, 94
spirit places 19–20, 22–4
stalactites/stalagmites see
  lithophones
Stanton Drew 104
stone circles 94–5, 104
  ICRL investigations 95–6
  "recumbent" 95, 96
Stonehenge 103–4, 120
  shaping on stones 103
Stones of Stenness 101
Sufis 63, 64

sweatlodges 90–1
synaesthesia 39, 56–9, 90
  sound-to-vision form 57–8

T

Tambaran (secret cult) 42–4, 45
Taversoe Tuick tomb 101–2
temples 31, 66, 144–8
  talking 141–3
tents, acoustics of 25, 28
Teotihuacán ceremonial city 144
Tiahuanaco pilgrimage centre
  143
Tikal pyramid 142
time, changing perception of
  33, 36
"time deafness" 65
Tomaros, Mount 18
tombs:
  ancient Greek 66–7
  chambered 101–2, 104
  megalithic 78, 79–86, 87, 88
    surveying 97–8
  see also cairns; passage graves
Tourist Information Centre,
  Coventry 54
trance states:
  body image in 22, 36
  music and 59, 139
  percussion and 47
  shaman's 21, 40
  theta rhythms during 48, 49,
    50
"trance-art" 107
trees:
  for Ashanti drums 42
  rousing spirits of 30
  "voiceful" oak 18
  see also forests
Trophonius, "voice" of 18–19
Tulúm temple 142
Tweneboa Kodua (spirit) 42

U

Umeda people 26

V

Valkoinen-järvi site 117
Vallée de la Grande Beune sites
  117

Vallon des Roches 116–17
velada (vigil) ritual 37
"virgin water" 140
vision-questing 20, 59, 139
Vitträsk, Lake 117
voices:
  ancestral 28, 115
  cult spirits 42
  of the gods 18–19, 142
  and intersensory perception
    58
  mimicking human 42, 43
  oracular 18–19, 143
  range/resonance frequencies
    80, 81, 82, 83, 88–9
  of rocks 119–23
  use in research 108, 109–10,
    112
voodoo 47

W

Wada Test 55
Warao Indians 39–40
water:
  divination by 18–19
  and echoes 117–18
  in Kaluli poetics 27
  Mayan use of 140, 143
  and rock-art 123
  spirits in 20, 139
West Kennet long barrow 93
Wayland's Smithy 79–80
"whispering galleries" 67, 148
whistles 109–10, 132–3, 134
whistling 32–3, 36, 141
Wintu Indians 20
words of power (*hekau*) 30–1,
  31, 32
Wovoka (Paiute prophet) 59
Writing Rock 139
Wupatki complex 144

Y

Yakut shamans 28
yawt (forest ogre) 26
Yirkalla Aborigines 28
Yokuts Indians 139

Z

Zion Wash site 139

< 160 >